MHRA
STYLE

NOTES FOR
AUTHORS, EDITORS,
AND WRITERS
OF THESES

FOURTH EDITION

LONDON
MODERN HUMANITIES RESEARCH ASSOCIATION

1991

First Edition published 1971
Reprinted (with amendments) 1973
Reprinted (with amendments) 1974
Reprinted 1976
Reprinted 1977
Second Edition 1978
Third Edition 1981
Reprinted 1984
Fourth Edition 1991

NOTE

The purpose of this handbook is to assist
authors and editors of academic publications, and
those preparing theses, to achieve clarity
and consistency in matters of style
and presentation.

*The first three editions of the MHRA
Style Book were edited and revised
by A. S. Maney and R. L. Smallwood.*

*This fourth edition has been extensively
revised and enlarged by a subcommittee
of the MHRA consisting of Derek Brown,
Alan Deyermond, Glanville Price (Chairman),
and Roger Walker.*

ISBN 0 947623 39 6

© Modern Humanities Association 1991
Printed by W. S. Maney & Son Ltd, Leeds, England

CONTENTS

7   DATES, NUMBERS, CURRENCY, AND WEIGHTS AND MEASURES

8   QUOTATIONS AND QUOTATION MARKS

9   FOOTNOTES AND ENDNOTES

10   REFERENCES

PREPARATION OF THE TYPESCRIPT

1.1 INTRODUCTION

This section is concerned with the preparation of typescripts for the press, either on a typewriter or on a word processor. For requirements relating specifically to the preparation of theses and dissertations, see Section 13.

If you are preparing to supply copy directly from a word processor or desk-top publishing system by means of tape, floppy disk, or modem it is essential to ascertain beforehand that your software, the medium chosen for transmitting or transporting the text, and any system of coding used to identify fount changes, accented characters, etc. are acceptable to the typesetter or printer.

1.2 GENERAL

Copy should be typed on one side only of good white paper, preferably A4. The lines should be double-spaced and the same type size and face should be used throughout. Ample margins should be left all round and the top quarter of the first page left clear. A good ribbon should be used, and the typing should be reasonably consistent in length of line and the number of lines per page. The first line of each paragraph (except the first paragraph of a chapter, section, or article) should be indented four spaces and the space between paragraphs should be the normal double spacing. The use of extra space between paragraphs creates much unnecessary work for the editor or printer. Do not use proportionate spacing and do not justify the right-hand margin of your text.

Some printers attached to word processors allow the use of several founts. Whilst the slanted, or italic, form of a fount may be used without additional marking to indicate italic type (provided that it is easily distinguished and used consistently), the bold form should not be used. (See Section 1.12.)

Whether you are using a typewriter, dot-matrix printer, daisy-wheel printer, laser printer, or other device, the selection of a suitable typeface is of the greatest importance. Typescripts employing typefaces with any of the following characteristics may be judged unacceptable and returned for retyping:

letters or figures (superior figures in particular) too small to be easily read

inter-letter or inter-word spacing which is either so narrow that letters run together or so wide as to interfere with reading

diacritics which touch the letters to which they belong

diacritical or punctuation marks which are too small or too faint to be easily read

script-like or eccentric typeface designs which do not permit high-speed reading

The most acceptable typefaces are those which closely resemble traditional typewriter faces.

The coarser types of dot-matrix printer produce results which are difficult to read at speed and therefore should not be used. Even with dot-matrix printers which produce otherwise acceptable results, care should be taken to ensure that accents and superior figures are clearly legible: if necessary, they should be inked in.

1.3   HEADINGS

Do not type headings or subheadings entirely in capitals and do not underline or italicize them, since either method may conflict with the style which the editor wishes the printer to follow. No punctuation marks (other than question marks) should be used after headings or subheadings.

1.4   NUMBERING OF PAGES

The pages should be numbered consecutively in the top right-hand corner and the total number of pages in the typescript should be indicated at the head of the first page. The author's name and address should be typed in the top left-hand corner of the first page and it is advisable for the author's surname to be typed before the number on each page. If any pages are removed or added during revision, all the pages should be renumbered in sequence throughout. Do not staple the leaves of the typescript together; a removable paperclip is preferable.

1.5   COPIES

The top copy should always be sent to the editor or printer. A good photocopy of the corrected typescript or, if that is not possible, a carbon copy carefully corrected against the top copy should be kept by the author. If the author's copy is to be produced by word processor, take care to ensure that it is identical to the printer's copy in every particular.

1.6   NOTES

Whether they are to be printed as footnotes or grouped together at the end of an article, chapter, or book, notes should be typed with double spacing throughout and should begin on a new sheet of paper at the end of the typescript. They should be numbered consecutively throughout an article or chapter, but not throughout a whole book, and each section should be headed 'Notes to Chapter [. . .]'. The notes will normally be set by the printer in type smaller than that used for the text;

they are therefore set separately, and should be kept separate in the typescript. Care should be taken to check that the reference numbers in the text are in their correct places and that they agree with the numbers of the corresponding notes. The reference numbers in the text should be typed above the line without punctuation (at the ends of sentences if possible) and the editor should encircle these numbers in ink when checking them; this is a considerable help to the printer.

1.7 SUBDIVISIONS

Major subdivisions within an article or chapter, if required, should be marked by increased spacing and the author should insert the words 'extra space' and encircle them. The first line of a new subdivision should not be indented. A convenient system for designating numbered subdivisions is to number all sections and subsections with arabic numerals and express them in series, divided by full points. This *Style Book* employs this system.

1.8 CORRECTIONS, INSERTIONS, AND COMMENTS

If corrections or insertions are brief, type or write them legibly above the line involved. Proof-correcting conventions should not be followed at this stage. The margins should be left clear for editorial use. If a correction or an addition is of considerable length, type it on a separate full-sized sheet and mark it, and the position where it is to be inserted, clearly (for example, 'Insert A, page 5'). Pages with extensive alteration should be retyped; the reverse of the page should never be used. Comments or questions for the editor may be noted in pencil in the margin so that they may be erased later. Special comments to be brought to the attention of the printer should be written near the top of the page, encircled, and preceded by the word 'PRINTER' (in capitals).

1.9 CHECKING

Typescripts should be carefully checked before they are forwarded to the editor or printer. In particular, all quotations must be checked against the originals, not merely against the previous draft; this checking must never be left until the proof stage. Though printers do not charge for correcting their own errors, they are entitled to charge for authors' alterations, and the charges for such corrections can be high. An editor has the right to expect that an author's typescript is final and authors should not be surprised to be informed that no author's alterations can be permitted on the proof or that, if they are permitted, the author must bear the cost.

1.10 LANGUAGES OTHER THAN ENGLISH

In languages other than English, accents and other diacritics may present problems to the printer and care should be taken with them. Accents which are not available on the typewriter or word processor should be inserted clearly in ink. Ligatures should also be indicated by hand:'ôê' for œ, etc. Other characters not available on the typewriter or word processor, for example the German double s (ß), may have to be similarly indicated.

If an author's work makes use of any characters which are not in normal use in English, attention should be drawn to this fact by a note attached to the typescript. It would be helpful to list the characters in question.

Authors who wish to make substantial use of non-Latin characters or transliteration should conform with the requirements of the editor or publisher for whom their work is intended. (For transliteration of Cyrillic characters, see Section 2.8.) The following publications contain much useful information on copy preparation and typesetting for languages other than English, both those using the Latin alphabet and others:

Hart's Rules for Compositors and Readers at the University Press, Oxford, 39th edn (Oxford: Oxford University Press, 1983), pp. 88–138

The Chicago Manual of Style, 13th edn (Chicago: University of Chicago Press, 1982), pp. 249–79

1.11 HYPHENS

If a line ends with a hyphen it may not be clear to the printer, particularly if the passage is in a language other than English, whether the word is to be set with or without a hyphen. When a broken word is not to be hyphenated, this should be indicated by curved lines (⌣) above and below the hyphen to show that the parts of the word are to be joined. For words not so marked the printer will normally follow copy and print the hyphen. This problem may be avoided by never allowing a non-English word to break at the end of a line. If a word must be broken, make sure that the way the word is divided follows accepted rules for the relevant language: the printer may take it as a precedent. (See also Section 2.3.)

1.12 TYPEFACES

The following alphabets may be available on a photosetting machine:

CAPITALS	SMALL CAPITALS	lower case
ITALIC CAPITALS		italic lower case
BOLD CAPITALS		bold lower case

These should be indicated on the typescript in the following manner: *italics* by single underlining of the relevant words or letters; SMALL CAPITALS by two lines under capitals or lower-case letters; LARGE CAPITALS by typing capitals or by three lines under lower-case letters; *ITALIC LARGE CAPITALS* by one line under ordinary capitals or by four lines under lower-case letters; **bold type** by a wavy underline.

Authors should note, however, that some photosetting systems do not offer true small capitals and that 'italic' is sometimes produced by slanting roman characters. In some typefaces the bold fount is very heavy and bold should be used in moderation, if at all.

Passages such as long quotations which are to be set in smaller type than the text, or with reduced leading, or indented should be typed to the normal measure and should be marked off by extra space above and below the quoted passage. A vertical line should be drawn in the margin against the quoted passage and the editor (not the author) should indicate the precise style of printing to be used for such marked passages.

1.13 ILLUSTRATIONS

For line illustrations, provide a clear original in black ink on white paper or board; for halftone illustrations, provide a glossy black-and-white bromide print. Indicate clearly on the reverse of each drawing or photograph the title of the book or journal, the author's name, the figure or plate number, and the size at which the illustration is to appear. (Be careful to write very lightly on the reverse of photographs or they may be spoiled.) Some reduction may improve definition, but excessive reduction may cause detail, such as fine lines or close shading, to be lost. Normally the original ought not to be more than four times larger, nor should it be appreciably smaller, than the required image. A decision concerning the size of the illustration should take account of the area occupied by the type on the page of the relevant journal or book, or any other grid into which illustrations are required to fit. If part of the illustration is to be omitted, indicate lightly on the reverse or on an attached paper overlay the portion which is to be masked off. Alternatively, the area to be masked off can be indicated on a good, full-size, photocopy of the illustration.

Indicate the approximate required position, relative to the text, for each illustration, but bear in mind that, for technical reasons, it may not be possible to place the illustration exactly.

Captions for illustrations should be typed on a separate sheet and attached to the typescript. Illustrations should be numbered in sequence throughout an article or book, plates in roman numerals, figures in arabic. Where appropriate, the scale of an illustration in relation to the original should be indicated. Acknowledgement of permission to reproduce the illustration, where appropriate, should be indicated below the caption.

Original illustrations should be very carefully packed to avoid damage: a strong piece of cardboard in the envelope is advisable. Do not use paperclips to hold photographs together.

1.14   RUNNING HEADS

Shortened headings may be required at the heads of pages after the first page of the article or chapter. It will assist the editor and printer if suitable abbreviated versions of titles are suggested.

1.15   CROSS-REFERENCES

Cross-references within an article or book should be indicated by typed zeros, encircled in ink:

See above [or below], p.⊙⊙⊙, n.⊙.

The typescript page number referred to should be pencilled in the margin and such cross-references should be carefully checked on the page proofs.

1.16   ORDER OF PARTS OF A BOOK

Before despatch to the printer the typescript of a book should be arranged in the following order (though few books will include all the items listed below):

Half-title (the full title, including any subtitle, of the book, and the title of the series and the volume number in that series, if applicable; the name of the author does not normally appear). The verso of this page is usually left blank when the book is printed.

Title-page

Bibliographical details (name and address of the publisher and printer, copyright, International Standard Book Number (ISBN), Cataloguing in Publication data, etc.). This page may be left blank by the author and the details supplied by the editor and printer.

Dedication or epigraph (the verso is left blank)

Contents list

List of illustrations (plates, figures, and maps, in that order)

Foreword (by someone other than the author)

Author's preface

Acknowledgements (if not included in the author's preface)

List of abbreviations and/or glossary if these are necessary to an understanding of the text; otherwise they may be placed towards the end of the book, before the bibliography.

Introduction (unless this constitutes the first chapter of the text)

Text

Appendix or appendices

Notes and references (for the whole typescript)

Bibliography

Index

If there is a frontispiece illustration it should face the title-page. The copyright should be indicated thus: international copyright symbol (©); name of holder of copyright; year of first publication. The name of the country where the book was printed must appear and may conveniently be combined with the printer's imprint. The preliminary pages, comprising all items before the main text, are usually numbered in lower-case roman numerals; though these numbers are not printed on certain pages (half-title, title, etc.), they are counted in the sequence. Arabic numbering usually begins on the first page of the text. However, since the page numbers cannot be added by the printer until the page proofs are prepared, all the pages of the typescript should be numbered in one (arabic) sequence throughout (see Section 1.4).

2 SPELLING

2.1 PREFERRED SPELLINGS

British spelling (as given in the *Oxford English Dictionary* and its derivatives) should be used. For verbs ending in *ize* or *ise*, the *ize* form is preferred. Some verbs and related words, because of their derivation, must have the *ise* spelling, e.g.:

advertise	comprise	devise	franchise	revise
advise	compromise	enterprise	improvise	supervise
apprise	demise	excise	incise	surmise
chastise	despise	exercise	premise	surprise

Note that the British spelling of 'analyse' and its derivatives has *s* and not *z*.

For other alternative spellings, the form given in the *Oxford Writers' Dictionary* (Oxford: Oxford University Press, 1990) should be used.

2.2 ACCENTS

The normal practice for foreign words which have passed into regular English usage is for accents to be dropped: thus accents are no longer used on 'denouement', 'levee', 'role', etc. But for reasons of pronunciation 'café', 'cliché', etc. retain their accents. (See also Section 5.6 and the *Oxford Writers' Dictionary*.)

2.3 HYPHENS

Hyphens should be used only when they serve a specific purpose. Apart from when they serve to avoid awkward sequences of letters (e.g. 'anti-intellectual', 're-enter', 'pre-ignition'), they normally indicate that two or more words are to be read as a single word with only one main stress. Note in particular such examples as the following in which the attributive forms have a single main stress and are therefore hyphenated while the predicative forms have two main stresses and are not hyphenated:

a common-sense argument	to lack common sense
a tenth-century manuscript	in the tenth century
a free-will offering	the problem of free will
a well-known fact	the facts are well known

Adverbs ending in *ly* are not hyphenated to a following adjective or participle:

a recently published novel
a highly contentious argument
a handsomely bound volume
a frequently occurring mistake

Collocations of certain monosyllabic adverbs (in particular 'ill' but not 'well' — see above) and a participle often have only one main stress and are therefore hyphenated even when used predicatively:

He is very ill-tempered.
Such a course of action would be ill-advised.

Note that, unlike the words 'early', 'late', 'north', 'south', etc., the prefix 'mid' always requires a hyphen (except where it forms part of a single word, as in 'midnight'):

The yacht capsized in mid-Atlantic.
a mid-June midnight flight
a mid-sixteenth-century chair
until the mid-nineteenth century
a late-nineteenth-century novelist
written in the early twelfth century

Hyphens should be used where necessary to avoid ambiguity:

two-year-old dogs   two year-old dogs
a deep-blue lake   a deep blue lake
to re-cover   to recover

The tendency is for a combination of words which constitute a single concept to come into use as a hyphenated compound but for the hyphen to be dropped when the compound is commonly used, provided that the resultant close (or solid) compound is not awkward to read. Thus we have:

backwater, battlefield, bookshelf, dustman, horsepower, paperback, paperclip, screenplay, subtitle

If a compound is in frequent use and is pronounced as one word with a single stress it is usually correct to write it as one word without a hyphen.

It must be admitted that there is considerable variation in the use of hyphens and it is impossible to formulate comprehensive rules. The best advice that can be given is to consult a good dictionary and to be consistent. (See also Section 1.11.)

2.4 QUOTATIONS

The spelling of quotations is always that of the book or edition referred to. But in quotations from early printed books the forms of the letters *i* and *j*, *u* and *v*, the long *s* (ſ), the ampersand (&), the Tironian sign (⁊), the tilde, superior letters in contractions, and other abbreviations are normalized to modern usage unless there are good reasons to the contrary, as, for example, in full bibliographical descriptions.

2.5   THE POSSESSIVE

The possessive of proper names ending in a pronounced *s* or other sibilant is normally formed by adding an apostrophe and *s*:

> Alvarez's criticism, Cervantes's works, Dickens's characters, in Inigo Jones's day, Keats's poems, Dylan Thomas's use of language

However, the possessive of 'Moses' and of Greek names ending in *es* (particularly those having more than two syllables) is frequently formed by means of an apostrophe alone:

> under Moses' leadership, Demosthenes' speeches, Sophocles' plays, Xerxes' campaigns

The possessive of names ending in *us* conforms to the normal rule:

> Claudius's successor, Herodotus's *Histories*, Jesus's parables, an empire greater than Darius's

Note that French names ending in an unpronounced *s*, *x*, or *z* follow the normal rule and take an apostrophe and *s*:

> Rabelais's comedy, Descartes's works, Malraux's style, Ramuz's novels

2.6   PLACE-NAMES

Where there is a current English form for foreign or other non-English place-names (Dunkirk, Galatz, Havana, Lampeter, Lisbon, Majorca, Moscow, Munich, Naples, Quebec, Saragossa, Venice, Vienna, etc.), it should be used. Rare or obsolete English forms (Carnarvon, Francfort, Leipsic, etc.) should, however, be avoided. In the case of Lyons, Marseilles, Rheims, the English forms rather than the French forms (Lyon, Marseille, Reims) should still be used in writing even though approximations to the French forms are increasingly used in pronunciation. The form 'Romania' should be used in preference to 'Rumania' or 'Roumania'. (For forms of reference to the place of publication of books, see Sections 10.2.1, 10.6, and 11.1.)

2.7   PERSONAL NAMES

Where generally accepted English forms of classical names exist (Horace, Livy, Ptolemy, Virgil), they should be used; obsolete English forms (Tully, Vergil) should be avoided.

Names of popes, Church Fathers, and saints should normally be given in their English form (Gregory, Innocent, Paul, Thomas Aquinas, St John of the Cross, St Francis of Assisi).

Names of foreign kings and queens should normally be given in their English form where one exists (Charles V, Catherine the Great, Francis I, Henry IV, Ferdinand and Isabella). Those names for which no English form exists (Sancho, Haakon) or for which the English form is quaint or archaic (Lewis, Alphonse, Emmanuel) should retain their foreign form. If in the course of a work it is necessary to refer to some monarchs whose names have acceptable English forms and some which do not, in the interests of consistency it is better to use the foreign form for all:

the reigns of Fernando III and Alfonso X
Henri IV was succeeded by Louis XIII.

2.8 SLAVONIC NAMES

Various systems exist for the transliteration of Russian and other languages using the Cyrillic alphabet. Contributors to journals, series, etc. in the field of Slavonic studies should ascertain what system is preferred and conform to it strictly. The MHRA specifies that the Library of Congress system without diacritics is to be used in all its publications in the Slavonic field, viz. the *Slavonic and East European Review*, Slavonic sections of the *Modern Language Review* and *The Year's Work in Modern Language Studies*, and relevant volumes in the 'Publications of the MHRA' and 'MHRA Texts and Dissertations' series.

Russian and other Slavonic names referred to in other contexts should, wherever possible, be given in the form recommended by the *Oxford Writers' Dictionary*, even when this conflicts with the Library of Congress system:

Dostoevsky, Shostakovich, Tolstoy, Yevtushenko

Note in particular that, except in the one case of 'Tchaikovsky', 'Ch-' 'not 'Tch-' should be used (Chekhov) and that the prime (') should not be used:

Gogol, Gorky, Ilya

(compare Library of Congress: Gogol', Gor'kii, Il'ia).

3 ABBREVIATIONS

3.1 GENERAL

Since abbreviations increase the possibility of confusion and misunderstanding, they should be used with caution. When writing for a particular publication, use only those abbreviations which are likely to be familiar to its readers. Never begin a sentence with an abbreviation, and avoid abbreviations as far as possible in passages of continuous prose. For example:

The author's comments on page 47, line 20, seem particularly apt.

Here the words 'page' and 'line', normally abbreviated in references, are given in full to prevent a disruptive effect in reading. Extensively used abbreviations should be clearly listed at the beginning of a book or in an early footnote to an article; the first use of an abbreviation should refer the reader to this list. (See Section 10.6.)

3.2 TITLES

Avoid inelegant or confusing abbreviations of the titles of literary works, especially in the text of your book or article. It is clearly necessary to avoid frequent repetition of a title, especially a long one, and discreet abbreviation will from time to time be needed. This should normally take the form of a short title, not initials: *All's Well*, not *AWEW*. Repetition can often be avoided in other ways: 'the play', when it is obvious which play is meant. In footnotes, and in parenthetical textual references in the main body of your book or article, abbreviations are more often appropriate, but they need not be inelegant and must never confuse. (See Section 9.2 on the avoidance of repeated footnote references to the same work.)

3.3 IN FOOTNOTES AND ENDNOTES

If possible, do not begin a note with an abbreviation which is normally printed in lower-case characters ('e.g.', 'i.e.', 'pp.'). If this cannot be avoided, the initial letters of footnotes should remain in lower case:

[21] pp. 127–39 *not* [21] Pp. 127–39

3.4 USE OF FULL POINT

A contracted form of a word, ending with the same letter as the full form, including plurals, is not followed by a full point:

Mr, Dr, Mrs, Ms, Mme, St, vols, nos

Other abbreviations take the full point:

M. (Monsieur), p., pp., a.m., vol., no.

Where the initial letters of each word of the title of a standard work of reference, journal, or series are used as an abbreviated title, full points are omitted:

OED, DNB, MLR, PMLA, TLS, EETS, ANTS

The full point is also omitted after the abbreviation for 'manuscript' in both singular and plural:

MS, MSS

and after initial capitals commonly used as abbreviations for countries, institutions, and organizations:

USA, USSR, UK, BM, BL, PRO, MHRA, UNESCO

3.5 OMISSIONS

Some words are abbreviated by omitting the first part of the word. If such abbreviations are in common use, no apostrophe is needed:

bus *not* 'bus
phone *not* 'phone
the twenties (i.e. 1920s) *not* 'twenties

3.6 AMERICAN STATES

Note that American states have both an official abbreviation:

Calif., N. Dak., Fla.

(a full point is used even when the abbreviation, e.g. 'Fla.', ends with the same letter as the full form, 'Florida'), and a postal abbreviation which in each case consists of two capitals:

CA, ND, FL

One or other of these forms (which may be found in the *Oxford Writers' Dictionary*) should be used consistently throughout the same piece of work.

Many of the official abbreviations (with some exceptions such as 'Mass.') are, however, obsolescent if not obsolete and the postal abbreviations will therefore be increasingly appropriate.

4 PUNCTUATION

4.1 COMMAS

In enumeration of three or more items, the words 'and' and 'or' should be preceded by a comma to avoid the possibility of ambiguity:

> The University has departments of French, German, Spanish, and Portuguese.
>
> *But:* The University has departments of French, German, and Spanish and Portuguese.
>
> You may travel by car, bus, or train.
>
> *But:* You may travel by car, bus or tram, or bicycle.

4.2 DASHES

Printers have at their disposal both a short and a long dash, neither of which is available on the typewriter. The short dash ('en rule') is used to indicate a span or a differentiation and may usually be considered as a substitute for 'and' or 'to'. It is represented in typescript by a single hyphen preceded and followed by a space:

> the England–Australia test match; the London–Leeds motorway; the 1939–45 war; pp. 81–101

Long dashes ('em rules') are used in pairs to enclose parenthetical statements, or singly to denote a break in a sentence:

> Some people — an ever increasing number — deplore this.
> Family and fortune, health and happiness — all were gone.

The long dash is represented in typescript by a double hyphen preceded and followed by a space.

Long dashes should be used sparingly; commas, colons, or parentheses are often more appropriate. Other punctuation marks should not normally be used before or after a dash.

A very long dash (——), known as a '2-em dash', is used to indicate 'ditto' in bibliographies and similar lists. It may be represented in typescript by a treble hyphen.

4.3 PARENTHESES AND BRACKETS

The term 'brackets' means 'square brackets', i.e. [ ], and is so used throughout this book. It should not be used with reference to parentheses, i.e. ( ).

Parentheses are used for parenthetical statements and references within a text. When a passage within parentheses falls at the end of a sentence of which it is only a part, the final full point is placed outside the closing parenthesis:

This was well reviewed at the time (for instance in *TLS*, 9 July 1971, p. 817).

When a complete sentence is within parentheses, the final full point should be inside the closing parenthesis. If one parenthetical statement lies within another, use a further pair of parentheses:

(His presidential address (1967) made this point clearly.)

This is quite unambiguous and there is no need to adopt the practice of using brackets within parentheses.

Brackets should be used for the enclosure of phrases or words which have been added to the original text or for editorial and similar comments:

He adds that 'the lady [Mrs Jervis] had suffered great misfortunes'.
I do not think they should have [conclusion illegible].
He swore to tell the truth, the old [*sic*] truth, and nothing but the truth.

(For the use of brackets around ellipses, see Section 4.8. For the use of brackets in references to the publication of books, see Sections 10.2.1 and 11.1.)

4.4 PUNCTUATION IN HEADINGS

Punctuation marks (other than question marks) should be omitted at the end of headings and subheadings. Punctuation marks should also be omitted after items in lists which are in tabular form (except, of course, full points used to mark abbreviations).

4.5 PUNCTUATION WITH ITALICS

There are italic forms of most marks of punctuation. The type style (roman or italics) of the main part of any sentence will govern the style of the punctuation marks within or concluding it. If the main part of a sentence is in roman but an italic word within it immediately precedes a mark of punctuation, that mark will normally be in roman. But if the punctuation mark occurs within a phrase or title which is entirely in italics, or if the punctuation mark belongs to the phrase in italics rather than to the sentence as a whole, the punctuation mark will be in italics:

Where is a storm more brilliantly portrayed than in Conrad's *Typhoon*?

In *Edmund Ironside; or, War Hath Made All Friends*, a play that survives in manuscript, we see this technique in operation.

Kingsley followed this with *Westward Ho!*, perhaps his best-known novel.

Who wrote *Who's Afraid of Virginia Woolf?*?

4.6 QUOTATION MARKS

See Section 8. (For the use of quotation marks with the titles of poems, essays, etc., see Section 6.3.)

4.7 EXCLAMATION MARKS

These should not be used in scholarly writing.

4.8 ELLIPSES

In quotations, it is important to distinguish between points that appear in the original, as in the following quotation from Samuel Beckett:

> Will you never have done . . . revolving it all?

and points indicating an ellipsis. While recognizing that this is an innovation in British usage, we recommend the practice of indicating an ellipsis by means of three points within brackets; the punctuation is retained when it is possible to do so:

> When, in the course of human events, it becomes necessary for one people to dissolve the political bands which have connected them with another [. . .], a decent respect to the opinions of mankind requires that they should declare the causes which impel them to the separation.
>
> Outside the hut I stood bemused. [. . .] It was a still morning and the smoke from the cookhouse rose straight to the leaden sky.

When the beginning of a sentence is omitted, the first word following the ellipsis is capitalized even if it does not have a capital in the original:

> A bugle sounded in the palace yard. [. . .] A man in the square started to sing the national anthem.

(In the original text of this last example, the second sentence begins: 'As though it were a call to arms, a man in the square [. . .]'.) (See also Section 8.6.)

5 CAPITALS

5.1 GENERAL

Initial capitals should be used with restraint; in doubtful instances it is usually best not to capitalize. Certain adjectives deriving from nouns taking initial capitals are not normally capitalized. For example:

Bible, biblical; Satan, satanic; Latin, latinate; Alps, alpine

Capitals must, however, be used for the initial letters of sentences and for the names of places, persons, months, days, and nationalities. They are also to be used for the titles of laws, plans, wars, treaties, legal cases, and for specific institutions and other organizations (the Modern Humanities Research Association, the Poetry Book Club). Capitals are used also for unique events and periods (the Flood, the Last Judgement, the French Revolution, the Peasants' Revolt, the Iron Age, World War II) and for the parts of books when referred to specifically (Chapter 9, Appendix A, Figure 8, Part II). Do not use initial capitals for the seasons of the year. Names of the points of the compass are capitalized only when abbreviated (N.) or when they indicate a specific area (the North [of England], South America) or a political concept (the West). The corresponding adjectives are capitalized when they are part of an official name (Northern Ireland) or when they refer to political concepts rather than merely to geographical areas (Western Europe) but not otherwise (northern England). 'Middle' is capitalized in such fixed expressions as 'Middle East(ern)', 'Middle Ages', and 'Middle English'.

5.2 TITLES AND DIGNITIES

Capitals are used for titles and dignities when these appear in full or immediately preceding a personal name, or when they are used specifically, but not otherwise:

The Archbishop of Canterbury and several other bishops were present, but Bishop Wilberforce was not.

When, after a first full reference, or with such a reference understood, a title is used incompletely but still with specific application to an individual, the capital is retained:

The Archbishop spoke first.

A word or phrase used as a substitute for, or an extension of, a personal name also takes initial capitals:

the Iron Duke, Alfred the Great, the Dark Lady of the Sonnets

5.3 MOVEMENTS AND PERIODS

Capitals must be used for nouns and adjectives denoting cultural, philosophical, literary, critical, and artistic movements and periods when these are derived from proper nouns:

Chomskyan, Erastian, Freudian, neo-Cartesian, Platonism

They should also be used for particular movements when the use of a lower-case initial might cause confusion with the same word in a more general sense:

a poet of the Romantic school
a novel with a straightforwardly romantic plot

Other words require capitalization when they are used to refer to specific historical periods (the Middle Ages, the Reformation, the Enlightenment, etc.).

5.4 TITLES OF BOOKS AND OTHER WRITINGS

In most modern European languages except English and French, and in Latin and transliterated Slavonic languages, capitalization in the titles of books, articles, essays, poems, etc. follows the rules of capitalization in normal prose. That is: the first word and all proper nouns (in German all nouns) take an initial capital, and all other words take a lower-case initial:

La vida es sueño; *Il seme sotto la neve*; *Autorenlexikon der deutschen Gegenwartsliteratur*

In English titles the initial letters of the first word and of all nouns, pronouns (except 'that'), adjectives, verbs, adverbs, and subordinating conjunctions are capitalized, but those of articles, possessive determiners ('my', etc.), prepositions, and the co-ordinating conjunctions 'and', 'but', 'or', and 'nor' are not:

Put Out More Flags; *How Far Can You Go?*; *The Man Who Was Thursday*; *All's Well that Ends Well*; *Pride and Prejudice*; *A Voyage towards the South Pole*; 'The Passionate Shepherd to his Love'

English works with foreign titles are normally capitalized according to the English convention rather than that of the language of the title:

Religio Medici; *Apologia pro Vita Sua*; 'La Figlia che Piange'

In French titles it is normally only the initial letters of the first word and of proper nouns which are capitalized. But if the first word is a definite article, the following noun and any preceding adjectives also take an initial capital:

Le Médecin malgré lui; Le Père Goriot; Les Grands Cimetières sous la lune; Un début dans la vie; Une ténébreuse affaire; Nouveau cours de grammaire; Histoire de la littérature française; A la recherche du temps perdu

However, for reasons of symmetry, capitals are sometimes used elsewhere:

Le Corbeau et le Renard; Le Rouge et le Noir

5.5 HYPHENATED COMPOUNDS

In titles and headings, capitalize the first part of the compound and capitalize the second part if it is a noun, or an adjective derived from a proper noun, or if it is equal in importance to the first part:

Non-Christian, Anglo-Jewish Literature, Seventeenth-Century Music, Vice-Chairman

The second part does not take a capital if it merely modifies the first part or if both parts are essentially one word:

Democracy Re-established

Elsewhere, words that would normally be capitalized retain their capital after a hyphenated prefix:

anti-Semitism, neo-Aristotelian, non-Christian, pre-Columbian

5.6 ACCENTED CAPITALS

Accents should be retained on all capitals in foreign languages if they would be used on the equivalent lower-case letters. The single exception to this is the French word *à*, which drops the accent when capitalized.

6 ITALICS

6.1 GENERAL

Avoid the use of italics for rhetorical emphasis. Any word or phrase individually discussed should, however, be in italics, and any interpretation of it in single quotation marks:

He glosses *pale* as 'fenced land, park'.

It may also be desirable to use italics to distinguish one word or phrase from another, as in Section 7.1.

If you are in doubt about whether to italicize a word, type it as though it were not italic and draw the editor's attention to it in a marginal note. It is easier for an editor to mark a roman word for italic setting than to delete an underline or to mark italic typing for roman setting.

6.2 FOREIGN WORDS AND QUOTATIONS

Single words or short phrases in foreign languages not used as direct quotations should be in italics. Direct, acknowledged, or more substantial quotations should be in roman type (in small print or within single quotation marks). Avoid the formerly common practice of using italics if such quotations are in Latin or medieval German; quotations in these languages are treated in the same way as those in other languages. (For the setting of quotations, see Section 8.)

Foreign words and phrases which have passed into regular English usage should not be italicized, though the decision between italic and roman type may sometimes be a fine one. In doubtful instances it is usually best to use roman. The following are examples of words which are no longer italicized:

avant-garde	dilettante	milieu	role
cliché	ennui	par excellence	salon
debris	genre	per cent	status quo
denouement	leitmotif	résumé	vice versa

(See also Section 2.2 and the *Oxford Writers' Dictionary*.) Certain Latin words and abbreviations which are in common English usage are also no longer italicized. For example:

cf., e.g., et al., etc., ibid., i.e., passim

An exception is made of the Latin *sic*, frequently used within quotations (see Section 4.3) and therefore conveniently differentiated by the use of italic. (See also Sections 10.1 and 10.3 on the use of such abbreviations.)

6.3 TITLES OF BOOKS AND OTHER WRITINGS

Italics are used for the titles of all works individually published under their own titles: books, journals, plays, longer poems, pamphlets, and any other entire published works. However, titles such as 'the Bible', 'the Koran', and 'the Talmud' are printed in roman, as are titles of books of the Bible (see Section 10.2.7). The titles of chapters in books or of articles in journals should be in roman type enclosed within single quotation marks; the titles of poems or essays which form part of a larger volume or other whole, or the first lines of poems used as titles, should also be given in roman type in single quotation marks:

Théophile Gautier's 'L'Art'; Keats's 'Ode on a Grecian Urn'; Shelley's 'Music, When Soft Voices Die'; Bacon's 'Of Superstition'

The titles of collections of manuscripts should be given in roman type without quotation marks (see Section 10.2.8). The titles of unpublished theses should be given in roman type in single quotation marks (see Section 10.2.5).

Titles of other works which appear within an italicized title should be printed in italics and enclosed within single quotation marks:

An Approach to 'Hamlet'

In the citation of legal cases the names of the contending parties are given in italics, but the intervening 'v.' (for 'versus') is in roman:

Bardell v. *Pickwick*

6.4 TITLES OF FILMS, MUSICAL COMPOSITIONS, AND WORKS OF ART

Titles of films, substantial musical compositions, and works of art are italicized:

The Great Dictator; *Il Trovatore*; *Elijah*; *Swan Lake*; Beethoven's *Eroica Symphony*; *Tapiola*; *Die schöne Müllerin*; *Goyescas*; *The Haywain*; *The Laughing Cavalier*; Epstein's *Christ in Majesty*

Titles such as the following, however, take neither italics nor quotation marks:

Beethoven's Third Symphony; Elgar's Introduction and Allegro; Piano Concerto No. 1 in B flat minor

Titles of songs and other short individual pieces (like those of poems; see Section 6.3) are given in roman and within single quotation marks:

'Who is Sylvia?'; 'La Marseillaise'; 'The Dance of the Sugar Plum Fairy'; 'Mercury, the Winged Messenger' from Holst's *The Planets*

7 DATES, NUMBERS, CURRENCY, AND WEIGHTS AND MEASURES

7.1 DATES

Dates should be given in the form '23 April 1564'. The name of the month should always appear in full between the day ('23' *not* '23rd') and the year. No internal punctuation should be used. If it is necessary to refer to a date in both Old and New Styles the form '11/22 July 1705' should be used. For dates dependent upon the time of beginning the new year the form '21 January 1564/5' should be used. When referring to a period of time use the form 'from 1826 to 1850' (*not* 'from 1826–50'), 'from January to March 1970' (*not* 'from January–March 1970'). In citations of the era, 'BC' follows the year and 'AD' precedes it, and small capitals without full points are used:

54 BC, AD 367

In references to decades an *s* without an apostrophe should be used:

the 1920s (*not* the 1920's)

In references to centuries the ordinal should be spelled out:

the sixteenth century (*not* the 16th century)
sixteenth-century drama

In giving approximate dates *circa* should be abbreviated as *c.*:

c. 1490, *c.* 300 BC

7.2 NUMBERS

Numbers up to one hundred, including ordinals, should be written in words when the context is not statistical. Figures should be used for volume, part, chapter, and page numbers; but note:

The second chapter is longer than the first.

Figures are also used for years, including those below one hundred (see Section 7.1). But numbers at the beginning of sentences and approximate numbers should be expressed in words, as should 'hundred', 'thousand', 'million', 'billion', etc., if they appear as whole numbers:

Two-and-a-half days went by.
Two hundred and forty-seven pages were written.
The fire destroyed about five thousand books.
She lived and wrote a thousand years ago.

Words should be preferred to figures where inelegance would otherwise result:

He asked for ninety soldiers and received nine hundred and ninety.

In expressing inclusive numbers falling within the same hundred, the last two figures should be given:

13–15, 44–47, 104–08, 1933–39

Note that an en rule (or short dash), represented in the typescript by a hyphen with a space on either side, is used without spacing between each pair of numbers.

Dates before the Christian era should be stated in full since the shorter form could be misleading:

Nebuchadnezzar (1792–1750 BC)
not Nebuchadnezzar (1792–50 BC)

7.3 ROMAN NUMERALS

The use of roman numerals should be confined to a few specific purposes:
a.   large capitals for the ordinals of monarchs, popes, etc. (Edward VII), and for major subdivisions within a text;
b.   small capitals for volume numbers of books (journals and series take arabic numerals), also for the acts of plays, for 'books' or other major subdivisions of long poems, novels, etc., and for certain documents;
c.   lower case for the preliminary pages of a book or journal, where these are numbered separately, and for minor subdivisions within a text.

7.4 CURRENCY

Words should be used to express simple sums of money occurring in normal prose:

The manuscript was sold for eight shillings in 1865.
The reprint costs twenty-five pounds.
The fee was three hundred francs.

Sums of money which are cumbrous to express in words, or sums occurring in statistical tables etc., may be written in figures. British currency before 1971 should be shown in the following form:

The manuscript was sold for £197 12*s.* 6*d.* in 1965.

British decimal currency should be expressed in pounds and pence separated by a full point on the line, not by a comma:

£12.65 (*not* £12,65 or £12.65p)

Sums below one pound should be shown thus (without a full point after 'p'):

84p, 6p, ½p

The same conventions apply to sums expressed in dollars or yen:

$500, $8.95, 25c, ¥2000

Where it is necessary to specify that reference is to the Irish pound or to the Canadian or some other dollar, an appropriate abbreviation precedes the symbol without a full point or a space:

I£, C$ (or Can$), A$ (or Aus$), NZ$

The abbreviations 'DM' for the German mark and 'fl' for the Dutch guilder (florin) also precede the figure but are separated from it by a space:

DM 85, DM 26.80, fl 100

Other currency abbreviations follow the figure, from which they are separated by a space; they are not followed by a full point:

Austria   Sch   (e.g. 200 Sch)
Belgium, France, Switzerland   F   (BF, FF, SwF where clarification is necessary,
    e.g. 95 FF)
Denmark, Norway, Sweden   Kr   (DKr, NKr, SKr if necessary)
Spain   ptas

The names of other currencies are best written out in full, at least on the first occurrence:

350 escudos, 2 million lire, 20 roubles

Despite the practice in the countries concerned, do not use the symbol '£' for Italian lire or the symbol '$' for Portuguese escudos, Mexican pesos, etc.

When written out in full, names of foreign currencies should be given in their English form where one is in common use, e.g. 'mark' or 'deutschmark' (*not* 'deutsche Mark'), '[Swedish] crown', etc. Note too the use of English plurals such as 'drachmas, pfennigs, schillings' (but '[Italian] lire').

7.5   WEIGHTS AND MEASURES

In non-statistical contexts express weights and measures in words:

He bought a phial of laudanum and an ounce of arsenic at a pharmacy two miles from Cheapside.

In statistical works or in subjects, such as archaeology, where frequent reference is made to them, weights and measures may be expressed in figures with appropriate abbreviations:

The priory is situated 3 km from the village of Emshall.
The same 13 mm capitals were used by three Madrid printers at different times.

Most abbreviations do not take a full point or plural s:

1 kg, 15 kg, 1 mm, 6 cm, 15 m, 2 ft, 100 lb, 10 oz, 1 lb, 4 l (litres)

But note that the abbreviation for 'inch' takes a full point to avoid ambiguity:

a hole, 7 in. in diameter

8 QUOTATIONS AND QUOTATION MARKS

8.1 GENERAL

Avoid the practice of using quotation marks as an oblique excuse for a loose, slang, or imprecise (and possibly inaccurate) word or phrase. Quotation marks should normally be reserved to indicate direct quotations, definitions of words, or similar functions.

In quoted passages follow the original for spelling, capitalization, italics, and punctuation (but see Sections 2.4 and 8.3).

8.2 IN LANGUAGES OTHER THAN ENGLISH

Quotations in languages other than English (including Latin and medieval German) are treated in the same way as those in English (see Section 6.2). Unless there are special reasons to the contrary, the forms of quotation marks in foreign languages (« » „ " etc.) should be normalized to English usage.

8.3 SHORT QUOTATIONS

Short quotations (not more than about forty words of prose or two complete lines of verse) should be enclosed in single quotation marks and run on with the main text. If, however, there are several such short quotations coming close together and being compared or contrasted, or otherwise set out as examples, it may be appropriate to treat them in the same way as longer quotations (see Section 8.4). If not more than two complete lines of verse are quoted but the quotation includes a line division, this should be marked with a spaced upright stroke (|). For a quotation within a quotation, double quotation marks should be used:

> Mrs Grose replies that 'Master Miles only said "We must do nothing but what she likes!"'.

If a short quotation is used within a sentence, the final full point should be outside the closing quotation mark; it may also be appropriate to alter an initial capital in such a quotation to lower case:

> Do not be afraid of what Stevenson calls 'a little judicious levity'.

> Carton's assertion that 'it is a far, far better thing that I do, than I have ever done' has become almost proverbial.

This rule applies even when a quotation ends with a full point in the original, and when a quotation forms a complete sentence in the original but, as quoted, is integrated within a sentence of introduction or comment without intervening punctuation:

> We learn at once that 'Miss Brooke had that kind of beauty which seems to be thrown into relief by poor dress'.

For quotations which are either interrogatory or exclamatory, punctuation marks should appear both before and after the closing quotation mark:

> The pause is followed by Richard's demanding 'will no man say "Amen"?'.
>
> Why does Shakespeare give Malcolm the banal question 'O, by whom?'?

When a short quotation is followed by a reference in parentheses, the final punctuation should follow the closing parenthesis:

> He assumes the effect to be 'quite deliberate' (p. 29).
>
> There is no reason to doubt the effect of this 'secret humiliation' (Book VI, Chapter 52).

The final full point should precede the closing quotation mark only when the quotation forms a complete sentence and is separated from the preceding passage by a punctuation mark. Such a quotation may be interrupted:

> Wilde said, 'He found in stones the sermons he had already hidden there.'
>
> Soames added: 'Well, I hope you both enjoy yourselves.'
>
> Hardy's *Satires of Circumstance* was not well received. 'The gloom', wrote Lytton Strachey in his review of it, 'is not even relieved by a little elegance of diction.'

8.4 LONG QUOTATIONS

Long quotations (more than about forty words of prose, prose quotations consisting of more than one paragraph even if less than forty words, and verse quotations of more than two lines) should be broken off by an increased space from the preceding and following lines of typescript. They should not be enclosed within quotation marks. A quotation occurring within such a long quotation should be in single quotation marks; if a further quotation occurs within that, double quotation marks should be used. Foreign forms of quotation marks should not be preserved unless there are special reasons for doing so.

Prose quotations, including the first line, should be set full out; verse quotations should be typed according to the lineation of the original and centred. These longer quotations should all be typed in double spacing and they should be marked by a vertical line in the margin to indicate that they are to be printed in the form which is standard for the publication concerned. When printed, a long quotation may be distinguished from the main text by setting it in a smaller size, indenting it, or a combination of the two. The preparation and marking of the typescript in the manner described would, however, be suitable for any likely style of printing (see Section 1.12).

Long quotations should normally end with a full point; even though the original may use other punctuation, there is no need (except for a question mark or exclamation mark) to preserve this at the end of a quotation. The initial letter of the first word of a quotation may also be changed to or from a capital if this is more appropriate in the context. A long quotation should never be used in the middle of a sentence of the main text: it is unreasonable to expect the reader to carry the sense of a sentence across a quotation several lines in length.

To assist the printer a long quotation should be marked with an encircled note 'verse' or 'prose' in the margin if there is any possibility of doubt.

Interpolations (indicating source) which necessitate the use of brackets in the opening lines of long quotations (see first example below) should be avoided. Such interpolations can almost always be prevented by including the first words of the quotation in quotation marks in the preceding text (see second example). But a little rephrasing will often eliminate the need even for this (see third example):

> This play [writes Dr Johnson, referring to *Cymbeline*] has many just sentiments, some natural dialogues, and some pleasing scenes, but they are obtained at the expense of much incongruity.

> 'This play', writes Dr Johnson, referring to *Cymbeline*,

> has many just sentiments, some natural dialogues, and some pleasing scenes.

> With reference to *Cymbeline*, Dr Johnson writes:

> This play has many just sentiments, some natural dialogues, and some pleasing scenes.

A reference in parentheses after a long quotation should always be placed outside the closing full point, and without a full point of its own.

8.5 QUOTATIONS FROM PLAYS

Where a quotation from a play is longer than about forty words, or two lines of verse, it should be treated as a long quotation (see Section 8.4). Whilst the spelling and punctuation within the text should be preserved, general rules may be applied to the treatment of speakers' names and stage directions.

Identify a long quotation by drawing a vertical line in the margin to the full depth of the quotation. 'Prose' or 'verse' should be written in the margin and encircled and, where a single quotation contains prose and blank verse, special care should be taken to indicate the point at which one ends and the other begins. Where a line of text is indented in the original, it should be typed as near as possible to its original position and the printer instructed in an encircled marginal note to 'follow typescript for indent'.

Most academic publishers have well-established conventions which should be observed when preparing a typescript. The following rules apply to MHRA publications in which quotations from plays appear.

Prose quotations are set full out with the speakers' names in small capitals, without final punctuation but followed by an em space. Second and subsequent lines of a speech are indented. Stage directions within a line of text are set in italic type within roman parentheses. If a stage direction immediately follows a speaker's name the em space preceding the text is placed at the end of the stage direction, after the closing parenthesis. Stage directions which occupy a line on their own are indented further than the text, and set in italic type without parentheses. No extra space is inserted between speakers:

BRASSBOUND   It will teach other scoundrels to respect widows and orphans. Do you
forget that there is such a thing as justice?

LADY CICELY (*gaily shaking out the finished coat*)   Oh, if you are going to dress
yourself in ermine and call yourself Justice, I give you up. You are just your uncle
over again; only he gets £5,000 a year for it, and you do it for nothing.
She holds the coat up to see whether any further repairs are needed.

BRASSBOUND (*sulkily*)   You twist my words very cleverly.

Verse quotations are usually centred on the text measure with the speakers' names positioned to the left of the text:

MACBETH   Prithee, peace!
               I dare do all that may become a man;
               Who dares do more, is none.

LADY MACBETH   What beast was't then
               That made you break this enterprise to me?
               When you durst do it, then you were a man;
               And to be more than what you were, you would
               Be so much more the man. Nor time nor place
               Did then adhere, and yet you would make both;
               They have made themselves, and that their fitness now
               Does unmake you.

In a book or article which makes extensive use of both verse and prose quotations from plays, it may be preferable to set the verse quotations full out but retaining the original lines of the verse:

CORIOLANUS   The gods begin to mock me. I, that now
Refus'd most princely gifts, am bound to beg
Of my lord general.

8.6 OMISSIONS

Omissions within prose quotations should be marked by an ellipsis (three points within brackets; see Section 4.8). Omitted lines of verse should be marked by an ellipsis at the end of the line before the omission, and not by a row of dots across the page. It is not normally necessary to use an ellipsis at the beginning or end of a quotation; almost all quotations will be taken from a larger context and there is usually no need to indicate this obvious fact unless the sense of the passage quoted is manifestly incomplete.

8.7 COPYRIGHT

It is the responsibility of an author to obtain permission for the quotation of any copyright material if such permission is necessary. Normally it is unnecessary to seek permission for the quotation of brief passages in a scholarly work.

It is not possible to give a definitive ruling to indicate when it is necessary to seek permission: copyright laws are not the same in all countries and publishers hold different views on the subject.

In general it may be said that the length of the quoted passage and the use to which it is put should be fair to the author and publisher of the work quoted in that nothing is done to diminish the value of their publication.

Complete items such as tables, illustrations, and poems must not be reproduced without permission.

9 FOOTNOTES AND ENDNOTES

9.1 GENERAL

(The term 'footnotes' is used throughout this section but the rules apply equally to notes and references printed at the end of an article, chapter, or book.)

Footnotes are an interruption to the reader and should be kept down to what is strictly necessary. They are intended primarily for documentation and for the citation of sources relevant to the text. They should not be used to provide additional bibliographical material on the general subject being treated, but not directly needed. Nor should they normally include extra expository material. Such material, if apposite and useful, is often better incorporated into the text or added as an appendix. Only after the most careful consideration should it be included in footnotes.

All footnotes should end with full points, whether or not they form complete sentences.

9.2 METHODS OF LIMITING FOOTNOTES

Simple references (such as line numbers or page references to a book already cited in full) can usually be incorporated in the text, normally in parentheses after quotations. A string of footnote references to the same text can be avoided by stating after the first full footnote citation: 'Further references [to this edition, etc.] are given after quotations in the text.' (See also Section 10.3.)

The number of footnotes can often be kept down by grouping together in one footnote references to several sources mentioned close together in the same paragraph. In particular, adjacent references to several pages of the same publication should be cited together in a single footnote. No footnote, however, should document references for more than one paragraph.

Footnotes should not repeat information already clear from the text: if, for example, the author has been named before a quotation there is no need to repeat the name in a footnote reference. If there is a bibliography to a book or article, footnotes can also be reduced.

9.3 POSITION AND NUMBERING

Wherever possible a footnote reference number should be placed at the end of a sentence so as to interrupt the flow of the text as little as possible; if this cannot be done, the number should be placed at a major break within the sentence (e.g. at a semicolon or at the end of a parenthesis). Only in exceptional circumstances should a single sentence have more than one footnote (see Section 9.2). Footnotes should be marked in the typescript by superior numbers, with no punctuation (full points, parentheses, etc.), in sequence throughout an article or chapter. (If a word processor is used, care must be taken to ensure that superior numbers are easily legible; see Section 1.2.) The author or editor should encircle the numbers in ink for the attention of the printer. A footnote reference number should follow any punctuation except a dash, which it should precede. It should appear at the end of a quotation, not following the author's name if that precedes the quotation.

A footnote reference number in the text should never be repeated to refer to the same footnote; if the same material has to be referred to again, a parenthetical reference in the text — '(see note 1 above)' — is the best method, though a new note using those words is a possible alternative.

Footnote numbers in headings and subheadings are to be avoided; an asterisk may, however, be used to indicate a general note to an entire chapter. A footnote number or asterisk should never be attached to the title of an article, because of the risk that bibliographers might include it in citations of the title. A note attached to the first or last sentence, or an unnumbered note preceding the numbered ones, will avoid this difficulty.

10 REFERENCES

10.1 GENERAL

References (in the body of the text or in footnotes) should document the information offered, to allow the reader to check the evidence on which an argument is based. A reference must therefore enable the reader to find the source referred to as quickly and easily as possible.

A work should be quoted or referred to in a satisfactory scholarly edition. If a work is published both in Britain and overseas, the British edition should be used unless there are special reasons for doing otherwise. If an edition other than the first is used, this should be stated. If an unrevised reprint is used (such as a modern facsimile reprint of an out-of-print work or a paperbound reissue of an earlier book), the publication details of the original edition as well as of the reprint should be given. Details of original publication should also be provided where an article from a journal is reprinted in an anthology of criticism (see Section 10.2.2): a reader looking for the article in a library is often more likely to find the original journal than the anthology. In referring to works of literature of which several editions may be available, it is often helpful to give the reader more information than merely the page number of the edition used:

p. 235 (Book III, Chapter 4)

Similarly, when quoting a letter from a collection, it may be helpful to cite the date as well as the page number:

p. 281 (23 April 1864)

Full references to well-known works (*OED*, *DNB*, etc.) are normally unnecessary, though for encyclopaedias and biographical dictionaries of multiple authorship it is often relevant to name the writer of the article cited.

It is usually necessary to give full publication details only on the first occasion a book or article is referred to; thereafter it should be cited in an abbreviated form (see Section 10.3).

10.2 FORMS OF REFERENCE

10.2.1 BOOKS

The first reference should be given in full in a form similar to that in the following examples:

(a) Tom McArthur, *Worlds of Reference: Lexicography, Learning and Language from the Clay Tablet to the Computer* (Cambridge: Cambridge University Press, 1986), p. 59.

(b) Carlos Fuentes, *Aura*, ed. by Peter Standish, Durham Modern Language Series: Hispanic Texts, 1 (Durham: University of Durham, 1986), pp. 12–16 (p. 14).

(c) Jean Starobinski, *Montaigne in Motion*, trans. by Arthur Goldhammer (Chicago: University of Chicago Press, 1986), p. 174.

(d) *Emily Dickinson: Selected Letters*, ed. by Thomas H. Johnson, 2nd edn (Cambridge, MA: Harvard University Press, 1985), pp. 194–97.

(e) *Approaches to Teaching Voltaire's 'Candide'*, ed. by R. Wildinger (New York: Modern Language Association of America, 1987), p. 3.

(f) *Boswell: The English Experiment 1785–1789*, ed. by Irma S. Lustig and Frederick A. Pottle, The Yale Edition of the Private Papers of James Boswell (London: Heinemann; New York: McGraw Hill, 1986), pp. 333–37.

(g) *The Works of Thomas Nashe*, ed. by R. B. McKerrow, 2nd edn, rev. by F. P. Wilson, 5 vols (Oxford: Oxford University Press, 1958), III, 94–98 (pp. 95–96).

(h) H. Munro Chadwick and N. Kershaw Chadwick, *The Growth of Literature*, 3 vols (Cambridge: Cambridge University Press, 1932–40; repr. 1986), I, p. xiii.

(i) José Amador de los Ríos, *Historia crítica de la literatura española*, 7 vols (Madrid: the author, 1861–65; repr. Madrid: Gredos, 1969), VI (1865), 44–54.

(j) *Dictionary of the Middle Ages*, ed. by Joseph R. Strayer and others (New York: Scribner, 1982–   ), VI (1985), 26.

(k) Hugo von Hofmannsthal, *Sämtliche Werke*, ed. by Rudolf Hirsch and others (Frankfurt a.M.: Fischer, 1975–   ), XIII: *Dramen*, ed. by Roland Haltmeier (1986), pp. 12–22.

(l) Debra Linowitz Wentz, *Fait et fiction: les formules pédagogiques des 'Contes d'une grand-mère' de George Sand* (Paris: Nizet, 1985), p. 9.

The information should be given in the following order:

1. *Author*: The author's name should be given as it appears on the title-page; forenames should not be reduced to initials. The names of up to three authors should be given in full; for works by more than three authors the name of only the first should be given, followed by 'and others' (see example (j)). If the author's name is more conveniently included within the title (as, for example, in editions of 'Works'), or if the book is an edited collection or anthology, the title will appear first (see examples (d), (e), (f), (g)).

2. *Title*: The title should be given as it appears on the title-page (although very long titles may be suitably abbreviated) and underlined to denote italicization. A colon should always be used to separate title and subtitle, even where the punctuation on the title-page is different or (as often happens)

non-existent. For books in English, capitalize the initial letter of the first word after the colon and of all principal words throughout the title (see examples (a), (f)); for titles in other languages, follow the capitalization rules for the language in question (see Section 5.4 and examples (i), (k), (l)). If figures occur in titles, these should also be italicized (see example (f)). Titles of other works occurring within the title should be enclosed in quotation marks (see examples (e), (l)). For books (usually older works) with alternative titles, punctuation before and after 'or' should be as follows:

The Queen; or, The Excellency of her Sex
All for Love; or, The World Well Lost

3. *Editor, Translator, etc.*: The names of editors, etc. should be treated in the same way as those of authors (as set out above) with regard to forenames and number to be given; they should be preceded by the accepted abbreviated forms 'ed. by', 'trans. by', 'rev. by' (see examples (b), (c), (f), (g)). For multi-volume works where there is more than one editor or group of editors involved, the information should be conveyed as in example (k); but see example (g) where only one editor is involved.

4. *Series*: If a book is part of a numbered series, the series title and the number (in arabic numerals) should be given (see example (b)). However, the name of the series may be omitted if it is unnumbered, unless the series title itself conveys important information (see example (f)). Series titles should not be italicized or put between quotation marks.

5. *Edition*: If the edition used is other than the first, this should be stated in the form '2nd edn', '5th edn', 'rev. edn' (see examples (d), (g)).

6. *Number of Volumes*: If the work is in more than one volume, the number of volumes should be given in the form '2 vols' (see examples (g), (h), (i)). Foreign equivalents, such as 'tome', 'Band', 'tomo', should be rendered as 'vol.' (see example (i)).

7. *Details of Publication*: The place of publication, the name of the publisher, and the date of publication should be enclosed in parentheses; a colon separates the place from the publisher, a comma separates the publisher from the date. Any detail of publication which is not given in the book itself but can be ascertained should be enclosed in brackets, e.g. '[1987]', '[Paris]'. For details that are assumed but uncertain, use the form '[1987(?)]', '[Paris(?)]'. If any detail is unknown and cannot be ascertained, the following abbreviated forms of reference should be used: '[n.p.]' (= no place), '[n. pub.]' (= no publisher), '[n.d.]' (= no date). Do not use brackets in a reference for any other purpose (for example, when the reference is already in parentheses), otherwise the impression may be conveyed that the information in brackets is uncertain.

In giving the place of publication, the current English forms of place-names should be used where these exist (e.g. Geneva, Vienna, Milan,

Munich; see Section 2.6). The abbreviated forms of names of American states or Canadian provinces (see Section 3.6) should be included if there is danger of confusion (e.g. Cambridge, MA; Athens, GA; Victoria, BC). These may be omitted if the name of the state or province appears in the name of the publisher (e.g. Athens: University of Georgia Press). For books published in more than one place, it is normally sufficient to refer only to the first. London and Paris should be included as places of publication in references unless (as, for example, in a bibliographical article) there are likely to be a great many references to books published at one place. In these circumstances, provide an early footnote in the form of 'Place of publication of all books cited is London [or Paris, etc.] unless otherwise stated'.

The name of the publisher (preceded by a colon) should be given without secondary matter such as '& Co.', 'Ltd', 'S.A.', etc. 'Press', 'Verlag', 'Editorial', etc. should be used only if the publishing house is not named after a person:

Éditions de la Femme; Harvester Press; Oxford University Press

It is not normally necessary to include forenames or initials of publishers, unless there are two or more with the same surname:

Brewer (*not* D. S. Brewer); Heinemann (*not* William Heinemann)

Where a publisher's name includes 'and' or '&', the conjunction should be given in the form which appears on the title-page:

Thames and Hudson; Grant & Cutler

A book which has more than one place of publication and a different publisher in each place should be referred to as in example (f).

Details of facsimile reprints of old books should be given as in example (h) where the original publisher is responsible for the reprint, and as in example (i) where different publishers are involved. Example (i) also illustrates the appropriate form of reference to a work published by its author.

A reference to a work in several volumes published over a period of years but now complete should state the number of volumes and give inclusive dates of publication and the date of the volume specifically referred to where this is not the first or last in the series (see examples (h), (i)). But if a work in several volumes is incomplete and still in the process of publication, the date of the first volume should be stated followed by a dash and the date of the individual volume being cited should be added in parentheses after the volume number (see example (j)). In some instances (for example, if each volume of a set has a different editor) it may be more appropriate to give publication details only for the volume cited.

8. *Volume Number*: In a multi-volume work the number of the volume referred to should be given in small capital roman numerals, followed where

necessary by the year of publication in parentheses (see examples (i), (j), (k)). It is very rarely necessary to insert 'vol.' before the volume number.

9. *Page Numbers*: If there is no volume number cited, 'p.' or 'pp.' should be inserted before the page number(s). It is customary to omit 'p./pp.' when the volume number is given (see examples (g), (i)), unless the page number(s) are also in roman numerals (see example (h)). If an entry relates to several successive pages, the first and last page numbers of the span should always be stated:

pp. 278–309 (*not* pp. 278 ff.)

If it is necessary to indicate a particular reference within a page span, the specific page number(s) should be given in parentheses (see examples (b), (g)).

Note that 'folio', 'recto', and 'verso' are abbreviated thus:

fol. 3^r, fol. 127^v, fols 17^v–22^r

10.2.2 ARTICLES IN BOOKS

The first reference should be given in full in a form similar to that in the following examples:

(a) Martin Elsky, 'Words, Things, and Names: Jonson's Poetry and Philosophical Grammar', in *Classic and Cavalier: Essays on Jonson and the Sons of Ben*, ed. by Claude J. Summers and Ted-Larry Pebworth (Pittsburgh: University of Pittsburgh Press, 1982), pp. 31–55 (p. 41).

(b) Fanni Bogdanow, 'The *Suite du Merlin* and the Post-Vulgate *Roman du Graal*', in *Arthurian Literature in the Middle Ages: A Collaborative History*, ed. by Roger Sherman Loomis (Oxford: Clarendon Press, 1959), pp. 325–35.

(c) R. P. Calcraft, 'The Lover as Icarus: Góngora's "Qué de invidiosos montes levantados"', in *What's Past Is Prologue: A Collection of Essays in Honour of L. J. Woodward*, ed. by Salvador Bacarisse and others (Edinburgh: Scottish Academic Press, 1984), pp. 10–16 (p. 12).

(d) Luis T. González-del-Valle, 'Lo interpersonal en *Presentimiento de lobos*: un estudio de los modos de transmisión', in *Estudios en honor de Ricardo Gullón*, ed. by Luis T. González-del-Valle and Darío Villanueva (Lincoln, NE: Society of Spanish and Spanish-American Studies, 1984), pp. 141–53.

The information should be given in the following order:

Author's name, exactly as it appears in the book (see Section 10.2.1, *Author*)

Title of article in single quotation marks

The word 'in' (preceded by a comma) followed by title, editor's name, and full publication details of book as in Section 10.2.1

First and last page numbers of article cited, preceded by 'pp.'

Page number(s), in parentheses and preceded by 'p.' or 'pp.', of the particular reference (if necessary)

A colon should be used to separate title and subtitle. For articles in English capitalize the initial letter of the first word after the colon and all principal words throughout the title (including the subtitle) (see examples (a), (c)); for titles in other languages, follow the capitalization rules for the language in question (see Section 5.4 and example (d)). The titles of works of literature occurring within the titles of articles should be italicized or placed within quotation marks, whichever is appropriate (see examples (b), (c), (d)). If quotation marks are used within the title, they should be double (see example (c)), since single quotation marks will already have been used to enclose the title itself (see Section 8.3).

If a particular page within an article is to be indicated, the full page-span should nevertheless be given in the first full citation and a reference to the particular page added in parentheses (see examples (a), (c)).

Reference to an article in a book which has previously been published in a journal should take one of the following forms:

> Alfred L. Kellogg and Louis A. Haselmayer, 'Chaucer's Satire of the Pardoner', *PMLA*, 66 (1951), 251–77 (repr. in Alfred L. Kellogg, *Chaucer, Langland, Arthur: Essays in Middle English Literature* (New Brunswick, NJ: Rutgers University Press, 1972), pp. 212–44).

> Edwin Honig, 'Calderón's Strange Mercy Play', in *Critical Essays on the Theatre of Calderón*, ed. by Bruce W. Wardropper (New York: New York University Press, 1965), pp. 167–92 (first publ. in *Massachusetts Review*, 3 (1961), 80–107).

The second form should be used if the collection of essays is more generally available than the individual journal (which may be old or obscure) or if reference is going to be made to several articles in the collection, thus facilitating the use of a short form for later references (see Section 10.3).

Other subdivisions in books, when separately cited, should be treated as seems appropriate according to this general pattern. Thus:

> *Troilus and Criseyde*, in *The Works of Geoffrey Chaucer*, ed. by F. N. Robinson, 2nd edn (London: Oxford University Press, 1957), pp. 385–479.

> Marqués de Santillana, *Infierno de los enamorados*, in *Poesías completas*, ed. by Miguel Ángel Pérez Priego, I, Clásicos Alhambra, 25 (Madrid: Alhambra, 1983), pp. 225–58.

10.2.3 ARTICLES IN JOURNALS

The first reference should be given in full in a form similar to that in the following examples:

(a) Richard Hillyer, 'In More than Name Only: Jonson's "To Sir Horace Vere"', *MLR*, 85 (1990), 1–11 (p. 8).

(b)   L. T. Topsfield, '"Jois", "Amors" and "fin' Amors" in the Poetry of Jaufre Rudel', *Neuphilologische Mitteilungen*, 71 (1970), 277–305 (p. 279).

(c)   Victor Skretkowicz, 'Devices and their Narrative Function in Sidney's *Arcadia*', *Emblematica*, 1 (1986), 267–92.

(d)   J. D. Spikes, 'The Jacobean History Play and the Myth of the Elect Nation', *Renaissance Drama*, n.s. 8 (1970), 117–49.

(e)   Robert F. Cook, '*Baudouin de Sebourc*: un poème édifiant?', *Olifant*, 14 (1989), 115–35 (pp. 118–19).

(f)   Eduardo Urbina, 'Don Quijote, *puer-senex*: un tópico y su transformación paródica en el *Quijote*', *Journal of Hispanic Philology*, 12 (1987–88), 127–38.

(g)   James Trainer, 'Sophie an Ludwig Tieck: neu identifizierte Briefe', *Jahrbuch der deutschen Schillergesellschaft*, 24 (1980), 162–81 (p. 179).

(h)   Maurizio Perugi, 'James Sully e la formazione dell'estetica pascoliana', *Studi di Filologia Italiana*, 42 (1984), 225–309.

The information should be given in the following order:

Author's name, exactly as it appears in the article (see Section 10.2.1, *Author*)

Title of article, in single quotation marks

Title of journal, italicized

Volume number, in arabic numerals

Year(s) of publication, in parentheses

First and last page numbers of article cited, not preceded by 'pp.'

Page number(s), in parentheses and preceded by 'p.' or 'pp.', of the particular reference (if necessary)

The use of the colon to separate the title and subtitle in an article, the norms for capitalization within the title and subtitle, the treatment of the titles of works of literature occurring within the titles of articles, and references to particular pages within an article are, as the examples illustrate, treated in the same way as for articles in books (see Section 10.2.2). Note, however, that the page span of articles in journals is not preceded by 'pp.'.

Only the main title of a journal should be given. An initial '*The*' or '*A*' and any subtitle should be omitted. If the journal title is abbreviated to initials, full points should not be used (see example (a) and Section 3.4). The titles of journals should be abbreviated only when the abbreviation is likely to be familiar to all readers (e.g. *PMLA*), otherwise the title should be given in full. If there are to be several references to the same journal, an abbreviated title should be indicated after the first full reference (e.g. *French Studies* (hereafter *FS*)) or in a preliminary list of abbreviations. For the proceedings of learned societies, etc., the name of the organization should be italicized as part of the title (e.g. *Proceedings of the British Academy*).

The volume number should be given in arabic numerals, no matter what the style preferred by the journal (e.g. *Medium Aevum*, 58, *not* LVIII). The number should not be preceded by 'vol.'. If a journal has ceased and then restarted publication with a new numbering, this should be indicated by 'n.s.' (= ' new series') before the volume number (see example (d)).

If the separate issues of a journal cover an academic year rather than a calendar year, this should be indicated as in example (f). If the publication of a volume of a journal has been considerably delayed, the actual year of publication should be given in brackets after the official year (e.g. 1983 [1987]).

Normally it will not be necessary to cite the month or season of publication or the part number of an issue of a journal, unless the part numbers are individually paginated, in which case the information should be given:

> Lionel Trilling, 'In Mansfield Park', *Encounter*, 3.3 (September 1954), 9–19.
>
> José Luis Pardo, 'Filosofía y clausura de la modernidad', *Revista de Occidente*, no. 66 (November 1986), 35–47.

10.2.4 ARTICLES IN NEWSPAPERS AND MAGAZINES

References to articles in newspapers or magazines require only the date of issue (day, month, and year) and the page number(s); volume or part numbers should not be included:

> Michael Schmidt, 'Tragedy of Three Star-Crossed Lovers', *Daily Telegraph*, 1 February 1990, p. 14.
>
> Frederic Raphael, 'France's Final Solution', *Sunday Times*, 19 February 1978, p. 40.
>
> Jacques-Pierre Amette, 'Thé et désespoir', *Le Point*, 8 October 1989, p. 18.
>
> Carlos Bousoño, 'La ebriedad de un poeta puro', *El País*, 21 May 1989, p. 17.

Note that only the main title of the newspaper or magazine should be given and that initial '*The*' or '*A*' is normally omitted when citing English-language publications, with the exception of *The Times*. The date of issue (with the month always in English) should be given between commas, not parentheses, and the page number(s) should be preceded by 'p.' or 'pp.'. Otherwise the method of citation is the same as for other articles (see Sections 10.2.2 and 10.2.3).

10.2.5 THESES AND DISSERTATIONS

The titles of unpublished theses and dissertations should be in roman type within single quotation marks; capitalization should follow the conventions of the language in question (see Section 5.4). The degree level (where known), university, and date should be in parentheses:

Robert Ingram, 'Historical Drama in Great Britain from 1935 to the Present' (unpublished doctoral thesis, University of London, 1988), p. 17.

Diedrich Diederichsen, 'Shakespeare und das deutsche Märchendrama' (unpublished doctoral thesis, University of Hamburg, 1952), p. 91.

Mary Taylor, 'The Legend of Apollonius of Tyre in Spanish and French Literature before 1500' (unpublished master's thesis, University of Manchester, 1977), pp. 45–47.

James-Louis Boyle, 'Marcel Proust et les écrivains anglais' (unpublished thesis, University of Paris, 1953), p. 22.

Note that American universities distinguish between a master's 'thesis' and a doctoral 'dissertation':

Barbara Jean Trisler, 'A Comparative Study of the Character Portrayal of Celestina and Other Golden Age Celestinesque Protagonists' (unpublished master's thesis, University of Oklahoma, 1977), p. 4.

William Eugene Simeone, 'Sir Richard Fanshawe: An Account of his Life and Writings' (unpublished doctoral dissertation, University of Pennsylvania, 1950), pp. 166–79.

If a published abstract of an unpublished thesis or dissertation is known to exist, the information should be given:

James Franklin Burke, 'A Critical and Artistic Study of the *Libro del Cavallero Cifar*' (unpublished doctoral dissertation, University of North Carolina, 1966; abstract in *Dissertation Abstracts*, 27 (1966–67), 2525–A).

10.2.6 PLAYS AND LONG POEMS

After the first full reference to the edition used (see Section 10.2.1), later references, wherever possible incorporated after quotations within the text (see Section 9.2), should be given as: *The Merchant of Venice*, II. 3. 10; *The Faerie Queene*, IV. 26. 35; *Paradise Lost*, IX. 342; *Aeneid*, VI, 215; *Samson Agonistes*, 1. 819 (meaning, in each case, that the line is the first line of the quotation). It is unnecessary to give a closing line number when a sequence of consecutive lines is quoted. The form 'IV. 2. 210–23' should be used when a passage is referred to but not quoted. If there are substantial omissions in the lines quoted, the form 'IV. 3. 412, 423', meaning that the quotation begins at line 412 and that there is an omission before line 423, should generally be sufficient. The omission will also be marked in the text (see Section 8.6).

Small capital roman numerals should be used for the numbers of acts of plays, and for the numbers of 'books' and other major subdivisions. Smaller subdivisions (scenes, cantos, chapters, etc.) and line numbers are usually indicated by arabic numerals. Figures in references should be separated by full points (not commas).

10.2.7 THE BIBLE

References should be in the following form: Isaiah 22. 17; II Corinthians 5. 13–15. Note that books of the Bible are not italicized; roman numerals are used for the numbers of books, arabic numerals (separated by a full point) for chapters and verses.

10.2.8 MANUSCRIPTS

Names of repositories and collections should be given in full in the first instance and an abbreviated form should be used for subsequent references. The degree of abbreviation which may be acceptable will depend upon the frequency with which a particular repository, collection, or manuscript is referred to. The names of manuscript collections should be given in roman type without quotation marks and the citation of manuscripts within collections should be according to the system of classification of the repository.

The following examples show the method of citation both for first and for later references. Note that, because of the danger of ambiguity, the abbreviations 'fol.' and 'fols' are preferred to 'f.' and 'ff.'. Note also the abbreviated forms for 'recto' and 'verso'.

First reference:	British Library, Cotton MSS, Caligula D III, fol. 15
Later references:	BL, Cotton MSS, Caligula D III, fols 17^v–19^r
or:	Cotton MSS, Caligula D III, fols 17^v–19^r
First reference:	Paris, Bibliothèque Nationale, fonds français, 1124
Later references:	BN, f. fr. 1124
First reference:	Sheffield Central Library, Fitzwilliam MS E.209
Later references:	Sheffield CL, Fitzwilliam MS E.151
First reference:	Public Record Office, Home Office, HO 42/196
Later references:	PRO, HO 42/196

10.3 LATER REFERENCES

In all references to a book or article after the first, the shortest intelligible form should be used. This will normally be the author's name followed by the volume (if applicable) and page reference:

McArthur, p. 62.
Chadwick and Chadwick, III, 72.
Elsky, pp. 42–46 (p. 43).

Sometimes, particularly in the case of editions of 'works' or collections of essays, a short-title form of reference may be more appropriate:

Boswell, p. 326.
Arthurian Literature, pp. 325–35 (p. 327).
Thomas Nashe, III, 96.

If no ambiguity is possible, the (volume and) page number should be given alone and preferably be included in parentheses within the text rather than as a footnote (see Section 9.2). Sometimes it may be necessary, for example when more than one work by an author has been cited, to repeat a title, in a shortened form:

McArthur, *Worlds of Reference*, p. 9.

If there can be no doubt which author is being referred to but more than one of his or her works has been cited, use the short title of the specific work followed by the page reference:

Worlds of Reference, p. 9.
'The Lover as Icarus', p. 12.

The phrases 'loc. cit.' and 'op. cit.' are likely to confuse the reader. Since they are only marginally more economical of space than the unambiguous repetition of the name of the author or the short title of the work, they should not be used. The term 'ibid.' should be used very sparingly and limited to those situations where there is no possibility of confusion, such as after a second reference which is separated from its predecessor by no more than four lines of typescript.

10.4 CITATION BY THE AUTHOR–DATE SYSTEM

The Author–Date System of referencing (also known as the Harvard System) is widely used in many disciplines, though it is still uncommon in literary studies. If conventional footnotes or endnotes are needed for expansion, clarification, or parallel discussion they should also be used for quoting references. A combination of conventional notes and the Author–Date System is unnecessarily cumbersome for the reader and should not be contemplated.

It should be noted that the Author–Date System is an alternative system to that used in MHRA publications and that certain aspects of it are therefore not consistent with the recommendations of Sections 10.2, 10.3, and 10.6 of this *Style Book*.

The Author–Date System requires all references to be placed in a bibliography at the end of the article or book. References in the text give the surname of the author and the publication date of the work to which reference is made. This information is enclosed in parentheses:

Certain alloys, when exposed to specific environments, fail under the continued action of low stresses (Swann 1981).

Some investigators (Fitton and Smith 1979; Brown 1980) have found that these theories have not proved reliable.

When it is necessary to draw attention to a particular page or pages this may be done thus:

> The building is not accepted as Anglo-Saxon (Taylor and Taylor 1965, 159–60, 283–84).

If two or more works by the same author have the same publication date they should be distinguished by adding letters after the date:

> Unmistakable evidence of a medieval field system was found here (Markston 1952b).

When the author's name is given in the text, it should not be repeated in the reference. In such cases, the reference either follows the name or, if this seems stylistically preferable, may come at some other point in the same sentence:

> Smith (1977, 66) argues that [. . .]
> Smith, who was known for his contentious views, replied (1977, 66) that [. . .]
> Smith regards this interpretation as 'wholly unacceptable' (1977, 66).

The list of references is arranged in alphabetical order of the authors' surnames. This reference list differs from a normal bibliography (see Section 10.6) in that the date of publication follows the author's name instead of following the place of publication, in that authors' first names are uniformly reduced to initials, and in that the initials of all authors follow the surname. This arrangement makes it easier for the reader to relate the textual reference (author, date) to the final list of references. Other points to be noted are:

1. The name of the place of publication of books need not be in parentheses but should be separated from the title of the work by a comma.

2. Titles of books or journals are printed in italics; abbreviated titles may be used for publications which are likely to be well known to the reader. Titles of articles are printed in roman type and are enclosed in quotation marks; some journals, however, no longer use quotation marks for article titles in the author–date system and authors should follow the practice of the journal to which they submit their material.

3. The words 'editor' and 'edited' may be abbreviated to 'ed.'.

4. If the work cited is an article in a book or journal the first and last page numbers of the article should be given.

5. If the list includes more than one work by the same author a long dash should be substituted for the name after the first appearance.

Examples are given below:

> Clark, N. B. and Wideman, R. F. 1989. 'Actions of parathyroid hormone and calcitonin in avian osmoregulation', in Hughes and Chadwick 1989, 111–26

Green, M. 1987. 'A votive model shield from Langley Oxfordshire', *Oxford J. Arch.*, 6, 237–42

Grew, F. and Hobley, B., eds, 1985. *Roman Urban Topography in Britain and the Western Empire*, CBA Res. Rept, 59, London: Council for British Archaeology

Hughes, M. R. and Chadwick, A., eds, 1989. *Progress in Avian Osmoregulation*, Leeds: Leeds Philosophical and Literary Society

Leech, R. 1986. 'The excavation of a Romano-Celtic temple and a later cemetery on Lamyatt Beacon, Somerset', *Britannia*, 17, 259–328

Stead, I. M. 1976. 'La Tène burials between Burton Fleming and Rudston, North Humberside', *Antiq. J.*, 56, 217–26

────── 1980. *Rudston Roman Villa*, Leeds: Yorkshire Archaeology Society

If unpublished documents are referred to, an abbreviated form of reference should appear in parentheses in the text and a separate list should appear at the end of the paper preceding or following the list of published sources (which may include unpublished theses and dissertations since they have specific authors). The items in the list should be arranged in systematic (e.g. alphabetical) order. The following examples illustrate, in the left-hand column, the abbreviations used in the text and, in the right-hand column, the full references:

BL Bib. Reg. 18 D III	British Library, Royal Books, Report to Lord Burghley on the western border, 1590
CRO, Probate	Cumberland Record Office, Carlisle Castle, Probate Records
NLS 6118	National Library of Scotland, Edinburgh, Armstrong MS 6118
PRO, HO 42/196	Public Record Office, Home Office, HO 42/196

10.5 CROSS-REFERENCES

Avoid, as far as possible, cross-references within an article or book. The page numbers in the printed article or book will not, of course, coincide with those in the typescript, and numerous references of this kind will therefore involve considerable extra work for author, editor, and printer, and will increase the possibility of error. Cross-references to pages can sometimes be avoided by giving references to chapters, sections, or notes, if the notes are numbered consecutively throughout each chapter or article: 'See Chapter 3', 'See Section 4.3', 'See Chapter 4, note 7'. (For the treatment of cross-references, if they are necessary, see Section 1.15.)

10.6 BIBLIOGRAPHIES

In an alphabetical bibliography the surname of the author or editor whose surname governs the alphabetical position will precede the forename(s) or initial(s). Do not reverse the normal order for collaborating authors or editors other than the first quoted. The following examples illustrate these points:

Johnson, Thomas H., ed., *Emily Dickinson: Selected Letters*, 2nd edn (Cambridge, MA: Harvard University Press, 1985)

Cook, Robert F., '*Baudouin de Sebourc*: un poème édifiant?', *Olifant*, 14 (1989), 115–35

Fuentes, Carlos, *Aura*, ed. by Peter Standish, Durham Modern Language Series: Hispanic Texts, 1 (Durham: University of Durham, 1986)

McKerrow, R. B., ed., *The Works of Thomas Nashe*, 2nd edn, rev. by F. P. Wilson, 5 vols (Oxford: Oxford University Press, 1958)

Chadwick, H. Munro, and N. Kershaw Chadwick, *The Growth of Literature*, 3 vols (Cambridge: Cambridge University Press, 1932–40; repr. 1986)

Strayer, Joseph R., and others, eds, *Dictionary of the Middle Ages* (New York: Scribner, 1982–   ), VI (1985)

Where many of the books cited in the bibliography have the same place of publication (e.g. London or Paris), this may be abbreviated ('L.' or 'P.') or omitted, but there must be a general note to explain this at the beginning of the bibliography. The titles of frequently cited journals or series should also be abbreviated (without full points) and a list of these and the full forms given in a list of abbreviations:

MLR   *Modern Language Review*
YES   *Yearbook of English Studies*

The system of abbreviations employed in *The Year's Work in Modern Language Studies* is widely used in the fields of language and literature. If the bibliography covers other areas, a system of abbreviations generally recognized within the field should be used.

In a bibliography in list form, final full points after each item should not be used. In a long bibliography of foreign books the native forms of the places of publication are sometimes preferable; and if formal bibliographical descriptions of books are being given, as, for example, in review headings, the spelling of the place of publication should be as given on the title-page (see Section 11.1). It may be helpful to state the number of text pages in a book at the conclusion of an entry; the length of an article will of course be clear from the citation of first and last pages as part of the entry.

Above all, it is essential to maintain consistency of styling throughout a bibliography.

PREPARATION OF BOOK REVIEWS

11.1 HEADINGS

There is considerable variation in style amongst journals. Many journals have their own style sheet or notes for contributors and/or include in the preliminary matter for some or all issues guidance on their house style. The reviewer should in any case study typical headings in previous issues of the journal for which the review is being written. For reviews intended for publications of the MHRA the following models of headings will help (note that, for practical reasons, information given in review headings differs in some respects from that given in references and bibliographies; see Sections 10.2.1 and 10.6):

(a) *Worlds of Reference: Lexicography, Learning and Language from the Clay Tablet to the Computer.* By TOM MCARTHUR. Cambridge, London, and New York: Cambridge University Press. 1986. ix + 230 pp. £12.50.

(b) *Aura.* By CARLOS FUENTES. Ed. by PETER STANDISH. (Durham Modern Language Series: Hispanic Texts, 1) Durham: University of Durham. 1986. 53 pp. £3.95.

(c) *Montaigne in Motion.* By JEAN STAROBINSKI. Trans. by ARTHUR GOLDHAMMER. Chicago and London: University of Chicago Press. 1986. xii + 348 pp. £25.50 (paperbound £12.75).

(d) *Emily Dickinson: Selected Letters.* Ed. by THOMAS H. JOHNSON. 2nd edn. Cambridge, MA, and London: Harvard University Press. 1985. xx + 364 pp. £7.50.

(e) *Approaches to Teaching Voltaire's 'Candide'.* Ed. by R. WILDINGER. New York: Modern Language Association of America. 1987. x + 206 pp. $30 (paperbound $16.50).

(f) *Boswell: The English Experiment 1785–1789.* Ed. by IRMA S. LUSTIG and FREDERICK A. POTTLE. (The Yale Edition of the Private Papers of James Boswell) London and Melbourne: Heinemann; New York: McGraw Hill. 1986. xxiv + 332 pp. £30.

(g) *An Edition of the Early Writings of Charlotte Brontë.* Vol. I: *The Glass Town Saga 1826–1832.* Ed. by CHRISTINE ALEXANDER. Oxford and New York: Blackwell for the Shakespeare Head Press. 1987. xxiv + 383 pp. £40.

(h) *Annette von Droste-Hülshoff: Historisch-kritische Ausgabe. Werke — Briefwechsel.* Ed. by WINFRIED WOESLER. Vol. VIII, i: *Briefe 1805–1838.* Ed. by WALTER GÖDDEN. Tübingen: Niemeyer. 1987. x + 345 pp. DM 118.

(i) *The Centenary Edition of the Works of Nathaniel Hawthorne*. Vol. XV: *The Letters, 1813–1843*; Vol. XVI: *The Letters, 1843–1853*. Ed. by THOMAS WOODSON, L. NEAL SMITH, and NORMAN HOLMES PEARSON. Columbus: Ohio State University Press. 1984; 1985. xviii + 785 pp.; xvi + 775 pp. $37 each.

(j) *Lessing. Epoche — Werk — Wirkung*. By WILFRIED BARNER and others. 5th edn. (Arbeitsbücher zur Literaturgeschichte) München: Beck. 1987. 478 pp. DM 38.80.

(k) *Werke und Briefe in drei Bänden*. By JAKOB MICHAEL REINHOLD LENZ. Ed. by SIGRID DAMM. 3 vols. Leipzig: Insel. 1987. 786 pp.; 958 pp.; 994 pp. DM 58 the set.

(l) *The Complete Works of Voltaire/Œuvres complètes de Voltaire*. Ed. by WILLIAM BARBER and others. Vol. XXXIII: *Œuvres alphabétiques*. Ed. by JEROOM VERCRUYSSE and others; Vol. LXII: *1766–1767*. Ed. by JACQUELINE MARCHAND, ROLAND MORTIER, and JOHN RENWICK. Oxford: The Voltaire Foundation. 1987. 343 pp.; 518 pp. £40; £60.

(m) *Théâtre québécois: tendances actuelles (Études littéraires*, 18.3 (Winter, 1985)). Ed. by GILLES GERARD. Québec: Université Laval. 1985. 246 pp. C$6.

(n) *Scenes and Machines from the 18th Century: The Stagecraft of Jacopo Fabris and Citoyen Boullet*. Trans. by C. THOMAS AULT. Ed. by BARBARA COHEN-STRATYNER. (Performing Arts Resources, 11) New York: Theatre Library Association. 1986. xviii + 146 pp. + 47 plates. $20.

(o) *Mariana Pineda*. By FEDERICO GARCÍA LORCA. Trans., with an introduction and commentary, by ROBERT G. HAVARD. (Hispanic Classics) Warminster: Aris & Phillips. 1987. 175 pp. £17.50 (paperbound £7.50).

(p) *Italo-Hispanic Ballad Relationships: The Common Poetic Heritage*. By ALESSANDRA BONAMORE GRAVES. (Colección Támesis, Serie A: Monografías, 108) London: Tamesis Books. 1986. 152 pp. £18.

(q) *The Resistance to Theory*. By PAUL DE MAN. Foreword by WLAD GODZICH. (Theory and History of Literature, 33) Manchester: Manchester University Press. 1986. xviii + 138 pp. £27.50.

Full points should be used to separate the different details of publication, except where otherwise indicated in the notes below. The information should be given in the following order:

1. *Title*: The title should always be given as it appears on the title-page (not as on the cover) and underlined to denote italicization. A colon should be used to separate title and subtitle, even where the punctuation on the title-page is different or (as often happens) non-existent. Note that German convention often prefers to separate the title and subtitle by a full point (see examples (h), (j)). Bilingual titles should be separated by an oblique (see example (l)). For books in English capitalize the initial letter of all principal words throughout the title, including the initial letter of the first word of the subtitle after the colon (see examples (a), (f), (n), (p)); for titles in other

languages, follow the capitalization rules for the language in question (see Section 5.4, and examples (h), (k), (m)). If figures occur in titles, these should also be italicized (see examples (f), (i), (n)). Titles of other works occurring within the title should be enclosed in single quotation marks (see example (e)). For books that are part of a multi-volume series, study examples (g), (h), (i), (l). Note that foreign equivalents such as 'Tome', 'Band', 'Tomo' should be rendered as 'Vol.' (see example (h)). Special issues of journals should be treated as in example (m) if they are given a separate title.

2. *Author*: The author's name (in capitals and small capitals) should be given as it appears on the title-page; this means, *inter alia*, that forenames that are given in full should not be reduced to initials.

3. *Editor, Translator, etc.*: Names should be given in full as on the title-page, preceded by the appropriate abbreviated form 'Ed. by', 'Trans. by'. The names of up to three editors should be given in full (see example (i)); for works with more than three editors the name of the first should be given, followed by 'and others' (see examples (j), (l)). Occasionally more information than simply 'Ed. by' or 'Trans. by' may be necessary (see examples (o), (q)). For books that are part of a multi-volume series where there is more than one editor or group of editors involved, study examples (h) and (l); but see examples (g) and (i) where only one editor or group of editors is involved.

4. *Edition*: If the edition under review is other than the first, this should be stated in the form '2nd edn', '5th edn' (see examples (d), (j)).

5. *Number of Volumes*: If the work is in more than one volume, the number of volumes should be given in the form '2 vols' (see example (k)). Foreign equivalents such as 'tomes', 'Bände', 'tomos' should be rendered as 'vols'.

6. *Series*: If a book is part of a series, the series title and the number (if any) should be given (see examples (f), (j), (n), (q)). For subseries within a larger series, study examples (b) and (p). Information about the series should be enclosed within parentheses; series titles should not be italicized or put between quotation marks.

7. *Place of Publication*: The place of publication should be given in the form in which it appears in the book: thus 'Firenze' (not Florence), 'Genève' (not Geneva), 'Wien' (not Vienna) (see examples (j), (k), (m)). Note, however, that place-names in non-Latin alphabets should be transliterated. The abbreviated forms of American states or Canadian provinces (see Section 3.6) should be given only where confusion might otherwise arise (see example (d)). These are omitted if the name of the state or province appears in the name of the publisher (see example (i)). For books with more than one place of publication, see examples (a), (c), (d); no more than three places of publication should be given. If the place of publication is not given in the book but is ascertainable, the information should be conveyed within brackets: '[Paris]'. If the place is not ascertainable, the form '[n.p.]' should be

used. Note that some of the practices for indicating the place of publication of books in review headings differ from those recommended for conveying similar information in references (see Section 10.2.1, *Details of Publication*).

8. *Publisher*: The name of the publisher is separated from the place of publication by a colon. Publishers' names should be given without secondary matter such as '& Co.' or 'Ltd'. It is not normally necessary to include forenames or initials of publishers (see examples (h), (j), (k)) unless there are two or more with the same surname, as for instance 'Edward Arnold' and 'E. J. Arnold'. Where publishers have more than one name, the conjunction should be given in the form which appears on the title-page (see example (o)). Words such as 'Press', 'Verlag', 'Editorial', etc. should be included if the publishing house is not named after a person (see examples (a), (c), (e), (l), (n), (p)). Note, however, that not all books published by universities come from a University Press; such books should be described as in example (b). Example (g) illustrates a special publishing arrangement. A book which has more than one place of publication and a different publisher in each should be referred to as in example (f). If no publisher's name is given, convey this by '[n.pub.]'.

9. *Date*: The date should always be that given in the book itself, no matter what the publisher's details accompanying the review copy may indicate. When more than one volume in a multi-volume series is being reviewed, the date should be given as in example (l) if the volumes appeared in the same year. If they appeared in different years, express the dates as in example (i), that is, separated by a semicolon. If the date of publication is not given but is ascertainable, use the form '[1987]'; if it is not ascertainable, use '[n.d.]'.

10. *Pagination*: If the pagination is continuous throughout the book, follow the pattern of examples (b), (j), and (m). Often, however, the preliminary material is paginated in small roman numerals separately from the main text; this should be shown as in examples (a), (c), and (f). If the preliminary matter is not numbered but is clearly separate from the rest of the text, the introductory pages should be counted (with the title-page or half-title, if there is one (see Section 1.16), as page i) and the total expressed in small roman numerals. When a work in more than one volume or two or more volumes in a multi-volume series are being reviewed, individual pagination should be given for each volume, separated by a semicolon (see examples (i), (k), (l)). The number of plates, microfiches, facsimiles, etc., if they do not form part of the normal pagination, should be given last (see example (n)).

11. *Price*: Prices should be given in the currency of the country of publication, using the abbreviations set out in Section 7.4 (see examples (b), (h), (m), (n)). The price of books published both in the UK and abroad should be given in British currency only (see examples (a), (c), (g)). For multi-volume works it should be made clear whether the price refers to each volume or to the set (see examples (i), (k)); where the volumes have different prices, the price for

each should be given, separated by a semicolon (see example (l)). If a book appears in both hardback and paperback editions, the price of each edition should be expressed as in examples (c), (e), and (o). If a book appears only in hardback or only in paperback, it is not necessary to specify the style of binding. If the price of a book cannot be ascertained, omit all reference to its cost.

11.2 REFERENCE TO THE AUTHOR

The practice of insisting on the use of courtesy or professional titles before the author's name in the course of a review is falling out of use. A reviewer should use the author's full name (as it appears on the title-page) at the first mention and, in a long review, possibly at the last. In the body of the review reference to the author should be by surname only.

11.3 INSTITUTION OF THE REVIEWER

The title of the institution should appear at the end of the review on the left-hand side of the page. It is not necessary to add the name of the town/city if that appears in the title: e.g. University of Leeds. In other cases the name of the town/city should be given: e.g. Trinity College, Cambridge; University of California, Los Angeles; University of Victoria, British Columbia. Exceptions are well-known institutions where no confusion is possible: e.g. Duke University, Harvard University, Collège de France. Always use the form of the title which the institution itself prefers: e.g. University College London (*but* Birkbeck College, London); University College of Wales, Aberystwyth (*not* University College, Aberystwyth); University of Illinois at Chicago Circle (*but* University of California, Davis). Universities in non-English-speaking countries should be referred to in the appropriate English form: e.g. University of Munich, University of Tokyo.

If the reviewer has no institutional affiliation, the name of his or her town of residence should be given.

12 PREPARATION OF INDEXES

12.1 GENERAL

All scholarly works longer than an article or pamphlet need an index. Without it, a book's or a thesis's utility is seriously impaired: the reader is hampered in comparing one section with another; someone who read the book a year before and who wants to consult a particular passage may be unable to do so; and anyone who needs to search many volumes for a particular type of information, and who cannot realistically expect to read them all from beginning to end, will usually ignore the unindexed book. A very detailed table of contents will partially fill the gap, but there is no satisfactory substitute for an index.

12.2 INDEX ENTRIES

All scholarly indexes should include subject-matter as well as names. It is much easier to compile a name-index, but the reader of a book on America in the 1960s who needs to know about mixed marriages or monetary policy, and who finds nothing in the index between 'Miller, Arthur' and 'Monroe, Marilyn', will feel cheated, and with good reason.

Headings with a substantial number of page-references should be subdivided: no one wants to look at all thirty-seven pages on which a person is mentioned in order to find the one that gives the date of birth. It is impossible within the confines of this *Style Book* to give detailed advice on the subdivision of entries; such advice will be found in Carey and in Collison (see Section 12.4). In general, avoid several levels of indention, since this would lead to ridiculously short lines in a two-column index. Subentries may often be advantageously grouped in a small block of type. Remember that apparently identical words that have different senses, or represent different parts of speech, must not be grouped in a single entry.

For some types of work (e.g. biographies, critical studies) a single index is normally best. For others (e.g. catalogues of manuscript collections) several indexes may be needed.

12.3 THE INDEXER

Every book is best indexed by the author, who knows better than anyone else what is important and what is trivial, or how much detail is needed in subheadings.

12.4 HOW TO MAKE THE INDEX

The traditional method is to use cards or slips of paper, and this is still the only practical method for a book or thesis prepared on a typewriter. Printers, however, find it difficult to work with slips of paper, though cards are acceptable. If you have used slips, the final version of your index should be typed on A4 paper, in single columns and — like any material intended for a printer — double-spaced. It is essential to check each entry in the typed version against your cards or slips. Only one entry or subentry should appear on each card or slip. Trying to economize by putting more than one entry on a card or slip makes it difficult or impossible to insert new entries or reorganize a complex main entry.

If a computer or word processor is used, it is normally possible to generate index headings by flagging words in the text.

All indexers — and especially those making their first index — need technical guidance that is beyond the scope of this *Style Book*. An excellent short introduction is G. V. Carey's pamphlet, *Making an Index* (London: Cambridge University Press, 1951). Much more extensive guidance is provided by Robert L. Collison, *Indexes and Indexing* (London: Ernest Benn, 1953). You will also find it useful to take the index to this *Style Book* as a model, though of course it is too brief to provide an example of each problem that will confront you. It will, in particular, show how to punctuate entries.

One important distinction that experienced indexers make, and that experienced index-users expect, is between substantial treatment of a topic throughout several consecutive pages (shown as, e.g., '28–32') and passing references to that topic on each of several consecutive pages (e.g. '28, 29, 30, 31, 32'). Special features such as pages with illustrations or with substantial bibliographical references may be indicated by bold or italic numerals, but such devices should be used sparingly, lest they distract the user. For inclusive numbers, use the convention specified in Section 7.2; e.g. '301–03' (*not* '301–3' or '301–303') but '1098–1101' (*not* '1098–101').

13 PREPARATION OF THESES AND DISSERTATIONS

13.1 GENERAL

The requirements of universities and colleges for the presentation and layout of theses and dissertations (hereafter, we use 'thesis' as an inclusive term) vary in matters of detail. The following general recommendations will be applicable to most literary theses, but should be supplemented by reference to the particular regulations and requirements of the university or college in which the thesis is to be presented; candidates must, therefore, be in possession of a current list of such local requirements before a thesis is prepared for presentation.

Few institutions require that a thesis should be presented in printed form, and the comments that follow apply primarily to theses which will be presented in typescript, produced on either a typewriter or a word processor. They are offered on the assumption that recommendations in earlier parts of this *Style Book* have been followed before preparation of the final typescript begins.

13.2 LENGTH OF THE THESIS

Local regulations vary considerably on the permitted lengths of theses and these regulations must be consulted and observed. The total length normally refers to the number of words in the main text and appendices, but usually excludes preliminary matter, bibliography, and index. If a text is being edited the word-limit normally excludes the text itself but includes all explanatory notes, glossary, introduction, appendices, etc.

13.3 PARTS OF THE THESIS

13.3.1 TITLE-PAGE

The title should be a concise and accurate description of the content of the thesis. The title-page should also give the full name of the author, the qualification for which the thesis is submitted, the name of the university in which it is presented, and the date (month and year). Many institutions have a prescribed form of words for the title-page, which must be followed. If the thesis is in more than one volume, the number of volumes should be given on the title-page of the first volume and later volumes should have their own title-pages with the particular volume-number specified. Pagination should normally be continuous throughout the volumes.

13.3.2 ABSTRACT OR SYNOPSIS

An abstract should be included even on the rare occasions when local regulations do not require it. It is helpful to the reader, and it can be included in such publications as *Dissertation Abstracts International*. Local regulations are often precise and strict about the position, length, and form of the abstract. It is frequently required to follow the title-page. Unless other regulations apply it should not exceed five hundred words. An accurate and concise summary of the organization and content of the thesis is normally required. The scope of the work undertaken, the method of investigation, the main divisions of the thesis, and the conclusions reached should all be described. The contribution made by the thesis to knowledge of the subject treated should be clearly stated, without either undue modesty or ostentation. Many institutions require that the abstract should also include a statement of the total number of words contained in the thesis.

13.3.3 TABLE OF CONTENTS AND LIST OF ILLUSTRATIONS

Any preliminary sections following the table of contents, chapter and appendix numbers and titles, bibliography, and index should all be listed in the table of contents, with page references. Titles should agree exactly with their wording in the main text of the thesis. The listing of smaller subdivisions within chapters is useful, and if the thesis has no index it is essential. Such subheadings should be listed in full, and consistently throughout all chapters and sections. If a thesis is bound in more than one volume, the contents of the whole thesis should be listed in the first volume; each subsequent volume should begin with a list of its own contents.

A list, or lists, of illustrations, diagrams, etc. should follow the table of contents and should also give page references. For any full-page illustration which does not form part of the continuous page numbering of the thesis, this reference should be to the number of the page preceding the item in question.

13.3.4 PREFACE, ACKNOWLEDGEMENTS, DECLARATION

A preface may usefully follow the list of contents. General assistance that you wish to recognize — from supervisor, librarians, friends, grant-giving bodies — should be acknowledged here. Acknowledgements of specific instances of assistance are frequently better placed in a note at the relevant point in the text; acknowledgement of permission to reproduce illustrations, quotations, etc. should appear with the material concerned. When a thesis contains material that the author has already published (or used in an earlier thesis), this should be indicated in a preliminary declaration. If the thesis is based on joint research, the nature and extent of the candidate's individual contribution should also be defined here.

13.3.5 LIST OF ABBREVIATIONS

Abbreviations (of titles, etc.) regularly used throughout a thesis should be listed, with a key, immediately before the first page of the main text (see also Section 3).

13.3.6 TEXT

Theses should be divided into parts, chapters, sections, and subsections as may be appropriate. The first chapter will normally take the form of an introduction, placing the thesis in relation to its general topic and to other work in the subject. Chapter titles and headings of sections and subsections should be factual, concise, and descriptively accurate.

13.3.7 NOTES

Unless local regulations specify otherwise, notes should be numbered in a single sequence throughout each chapter (or section), but with a separate sequence for each chapter. The note reference numbers within the text should be typed above the line without punctuation. It is helpful to the reader if notes are placed, in reduced spacing, at the foot of the relevant page. This may be difficult in a typed thesis, unless you use a professional typist, but it is much easier on a word processor. If you cannot place notes at the foot of a page, they may be placed at the end of the chapter. It is better not to place them all at the end of the thesis. The choice should be made with regard to the nature of the thesis, the method of production, local regulations, and the supervisor's advice.

13.3.8 APPENDICES

Material, such as lists, tables, copies of documents, and other supporting information, which would constitute too great an interruption of the main text and which is too extensive to be included in the notes, may sometimes be offered in one or more appendices. (The proliferation of appendices, however, and the inclusion of material of doubtful relevance, are to be avoided.)

13.3.9 BIBLIOGRAPHY

Every literary thesis must contain a bibliography. This should not be compiled as a last-minute task before submission of the thesis, but will develop from the material being listed, consulted, and used while work is in progress. The degree of inclusiveness of a bibliography is a matter for careful consideration and consultation with a supervisor: it should include all works found relevant, and must detail all works referred to in the text. Full publication details will be included (see Section 10.6). The list will normally be in alphabetical order of authors, though in certain theses a chronological, or some other, order may be more appropriate. Some degree of subdivision within the bibliography is frequently desirable. Manuscript and printed material should always be separately listed. Other subdivisions might be into primary and secondary sources, general works and special studies, or any other arrangement that may be appropriate.

It is advisable to hold a bibliography in card-index form until the latest possible moment before typing, so that rearrangements and additions can be made. Never include more than one item on a single card.

13.3.10 INDEX

Although not always required by local regulations, the provision of an index of names and subjects is highly desirable, particularly for theses covering a wide range of material or concerned with the work of several authors. An index also is best held in card form until the latest possible moment; page references may then be added to cards when the final typing of the text is complete (see Section 12).

13.4 PREPARATION OF THE FINAL TYPESCRIPT

13.4.1 GENERAL

Adequate time must be allowed for preparation, typing, checking, correction, and (where necessary) retyping. The typing should commence as soon as possible since a thesis in a unique manuscript (or draft typescript) bears a serious risk of loss. If sections are being put into their final form as composition of the thesis proceeds, fair copies should be made as each section is completed. An entire thesis should never be given to a typist without some provision for checking while typing is in progress. Immediate examination of the first sections typed is essential so that recurrent problems and difficulties can be identified and prevented in later stages. Before any section of a thesis is handed over to a typist, all references and quotations should be verified and a thorough check made of the sequence of footnote numbers, both of the reference numbers in the text and of the numbers of the notes themselves.

13.4.2 PAPER, TYPEFACE, AND MARGINS

Unless local regulations specify otherwise, theses should be typed on one side only of white paper of A4 size and good quality. Both 'pica' and 'elite' type sizes are normally acceptable, provided that typing is of even size throughout and characters clear and black. Margins should be 4 cm (1½ in.) wide at the left-hand side (for binding) and 2 cm (¾ in.) on the other three sides. The typing should be reasonably consistent in the length of line and the number of lines per page. If a typewriter or word processor has an italic typeface this may be used for titles, foreign words and phrases, etc. (see Section 6), but underlining is normally acceptable.

13.4.3 SPACING

The text, preliminaries, and appendices should be typed in double spacing throughout. Single spacing should be used for inset quotations (see Section 8) and for footnotes; it is usually best for endnotes also. The bibliography and index will probably require a special tabular presentation; double spacing between items and single spacing within items is often a convenient layout here.

E

13.4.4 PAGINATION

Unless local regulations stipulate otherwise, page numbers should begin on the first page of the main text (following the preliminaries) and continue to the end, and should be placed at the top right of each page.

13.4.5 HEADINGS AND SUBHEADINGS

Chapters (and other main sections) should always begin on a new page; their titles should be in capitals and centred. Subsections should not begin on a new page, but should be marked by extra spacing; more important subheadings should be on a separate line and in capitals, but set over to the left-hand margin; minor subheadings, also set to the left and on a separate line, should have only initial capitals and should be underlined. If a system of designation is required for subsections, one based on the system described in Section 1.7 may be used.

13.4.6 CHECKING AND CORRECTION

Thorough checking of the final typescript is essential. It should be checked word for word and letter for letter against the verified copy given to the typist; quotations and references should again be checked against the originals; note numbers should be checked; and the typescript should be read through at least once more, preferably by a friend or colleague as well as the author. Only the smallest corrections should be made by hand (in black ink); all corrections of more than a letter or so should be typed in. Some corrections may well involve the retyping of a whole page, or more, and adequate time must therefore be allowed for checking and correction. Remember that you, not the typist, are responsible for ensuring the accuracy of your thesis.

13.4.7 CROSS-REFERENCES

Unless a thesis is divided into many small subsections, page numbers will normally be essential for cross-references. These cannot, therefore, be included until typing and pagination are complete. The author, however, will normally be able to guess whether a two-digit or three-digit number has to be inserted, and should make it clear to the typist how many spaces have to be left for the number to be typed in at the final stage. Since the task of inserting cross-references is troublesome, they should be kept to an absolute minimum. If the need for frequent cross-referencing emerges during the earlier stages of composition of a thesis, the overall structure may be at fault and a remedy should be sought before the preparation of the final typescript.

13.4.8 ILLUSTRATIONS AND TABLES

Illustrations (especially photographic plates, and tables or large illustrations which have to be folded) may cause difficulties with binding; the advice of the binder should be sought at an early stage if illustrations are likely to be numerous. Local requirements for the mounting of illustrations should be carefully observed; a binding margin of at least the usual 4 cm (1½ in.) will be required. If possible, illustrations should be inserted in the thesis near the relevant portion of the text. There should be a separate numbering sequence for each category of illustration (plates, figures, tables, etc.). Numbers and captions should appear below the illustration. If an illustration or table has to be turned in order to be mounted on A4 paper, its left-hand side should be to the bottom of the page of the bound thesis. The process of obtaining several copies of an illustration can be surprisingly slow, and adequate time must be allowed.

13.4.9 NUMBER OF COPIES

Local regulations vary on the number of copies of a thesis to be presented and on whether one copy is returned to the candidate after the thesis has been examined. All copies, by whatever method they are produced, must be identical.

13.5 BINDING

Nearly every university and college requires that theses should be bound in boards; some require this binding to be delayed until after the thesis has been examined, others require binding to be completed before submission. Local regulations on the style of binding and on the lettering on the front board (if any) and the spine (usually at least the name of the candidate, the degree, and the year) must be observed. Binding delays are frequent, and adequate time must be allowed.

13.6 PERMISSION TO CONSULT AND COPY

Many universities and colleges now require the authors of theses deposited in their libraries to sign a declaration granting to the librarian the right to permit, without further reference to the author, consultation of the thesis and the making of single copies (for study purposes, and subject to the usual conventions of scholarly acknowledgement) of all or of parts of it. As always it is essential to be aware of current regulations in the institution to which the thesis is being submitted.

13.7 FURTHER READING

The following may be found useful:

BS4821: Recommendations for the Presentation of Theses (London: British Standards Institution, 1972)

Barzun, Jacques, and Henry F. Graff, The Modern Researcher, rev. edn (New York: Harcourt, Brace & World, 1970)

Watson, George, The Literary Thesis: A Guide to Research (London: Longman, 1970)

E*

14 GLOSSARY

The entries include only those words which are likely to be useful to an author or editor. The glossary does not purport to be a complete list of printers' technical terms.

A4: a standard paper size, 297 × 210 mm.

art paper: a smooth, coated paper particularly suitable for printing fine screen halftone illustrations.

ascender: the vertical part of a lower-case letter, such as *b* or *h*, which extends above the x-height of the character.

ASCII: American Standard Code for Information Interchange: the code most commonly employed in computers, word processors, and phototypesetting systems to identify text characters.

ASPIC: Author's Symbolic Pre-press Interfacing Code: a type of generic coding which has gained some acceptance as a standard among publishers and printers.

base-line: the horizontal line on which all letters which do not have descenders appear to stand.

bleed: if an illustration runs slightly beyond the edge of a page so that a small part is cut away when the book is trimmed, it is said to bleed, or to be bled off.

bold: heavyweight type related in appearance to a specific roman typeface. This book is set in Sabon. **This is Sabon bold.**

brackets: used alone, square brackets [ ]. Other forms of brackets are: parentheses ( ), angled brackets <>, and braces { }.

camera copy: artwork, typesetting, etc. ready to be photographed for reproduction.

caps: capital letters. See also *small caps.*

caret: a sign marking the place in a text where additional material is to be inserted.

copy: material, usually in the form of manuscript or typescript, to be typeset or otherwise prepared for printing.

copy proof: a photographic method for producing single prints, enlarged or reduced in size if necessary, of line or halftone subjects. It offers a convenient but inferior means of incorporating illustrations into a publication without working with a separate negative for each illustration. The same process is sometimes referred to as pmt or photo-mechanical transfer.

cropping: see *masking.*

daisy-wheel printer: a machine which may be attached to a computer or word processor to produce output similar to that of an electric typewriter.

descender: the part of a lower-case letter, such as *q* or *y*, which extends below the base-line of the character.

desk-top publishing: the production of books and other publications using desk-top equipment operated by the author or editor as a substitute for all or part of the traditional printing process. Such equipment commonly has facilities for pagination and the integration of illustrations with text.

diacritical marks: accents, bars, dots, etc. printed above or below letters.

dot-matrix printer: a machine attached to a computer or word processor which prints letters and graphics as arrangements of small dots.

elite: see *pitch.*

ellipsis: three spaced points used to indicate an omission.

em: the square of any type size; therefore an em in 8-point type is 8 points wide. The type areas for a page are traditionally calculated in 12-point (pica) ems (see *point* below).

em rule: a rule which is one em wide, a long dash.

en: half the width of an em; also used in casting-off (estimating the length of a manuscript) to mean the average width of all characters and spaces, although this may not be equal to an en of the type size.

en rule: a rule which is one en wide, a short dash.

endmatter: material following the text proper, including appendices, bibliographies, indexes, etc.

endnotes: notes which appear at the end of chapters or at the end of a book, as opposed to footnotes.

epigraph: a short quotation, not essential to the argument, set at the beginning of an article below the title to prepare the reader for what is to come. Traditionally positioned to the right of centre.

figure: an illustration printed with the text (plates are usually grouped separately).

filmsetter: see *photosetter.*

floppy disk: flexible magnetic disk used in computers, word processors, and photosetting systems to store and transport encoded programs and text.

foldout: a leaf larger than the normal page size which is folded to fit within the size of the book. It usually displays a large illustration or table.

folio: (1) a sheet of manuscript or typescript; (2) a page-number in a book; (3) a standard-size sheet folded in half, hence a book of this size.

format: the page size and shape of a book: sometimes loosely used to denote also the design.

fount: (pronounced 'font') a set of type characters of the same design. It may include capitals, small capitals, lower case, numerals, and punctuation marks.

full out: see *set full out.*

full point: printer's term for a period or full stop.

galley proof: a proof of text divided into lengths, usually of more than page depth, for convenience of handling. Galley proofs are normally presented as a first proof so that all substantial corrections can be made before pagination.

generic coding: a means of conveying the structure of a text and features within it when photosetting directly from word-processor output. Specified character combinations are used in place of such things as fount changes, indentions, and unusual accents. A generic code may be devised jointly by the publisher and printer of a work or may be standard (e.g. ASPIC).

guillemets: quotation marks used in French and some other languages (« »).

halftone: a process whereby an illustration is photographically broken up into a fine grid of dots of varying size. When printed this simulates the varying tones of the original.

hard disk: large-capacity magnetic disk used in computers, word processors, and photosetting systems to store encoded information. Hard disks are not easily removed and are not used to transport text.

hot-metal typesetting: the setting and casting of type by machines using molten metal.

imposition: the arrangement of pages on a printing plate so that when the printed sheet is folded into a signature the pages appear in the correct order.

inferior: small numeral or other character printed below or partly below the base-line of the normal characters in the text.

ISBN: International Standard Book Number: a number which identifies a particular book in accordance with an international system.

ISSN: International Standard Serial Number: a number which identifies a serial publication, such as a journal or yearbook, in accordance with an international system.

italic: sloping type, as compared with upright, roman, type. *This is italic.*

justify: to space out lines of type to a particular measure by varying the space between words.

landscape: a book or part of a book (e.g. an illustration or a table) which has a width greater than its height. See also *portrait.*

laser printer: a device which may be attached to a computer or to a photosetting system, and which mimics the output of a photosetter to a degree limited by its electrostatic method of inscribing characters.

leaders: a row of evenly spaced dots designed to lead the reader's eye from one column of words or figures to another.

leading: interlinear spacing which is additional to the nominal body size of the type. For example, 10/12 Times is 10-point Times with two points leading. (The term is derived from lead alloy used for casting metal type.)

letterpress: the process of printing from raised surfaces such as type and engraved blocks.

letterspacing: the insertion of very thin spaces between the letters of a word. This is normally done only if the word is in capitals or small capitals.

ligature: two or more letters joined together as a single unit; common examples are fi, fl, æ, and œ.

line drawing: a drawing which has no variation of tone or shade but consists only of monotone lines and solids.

lining figures: arabic numerals of constant height, e.g. 1234567, as opposed to non-lining (or old style) figures, e.g. 1234567.

lithography: a process of printing based on the mutual repulsion of grease and water. The printing surface is not raised, as in letterpress printing, but is a flat image laid down on a grained stone or plate. A film of water is applied which covers the surface of the stone or plate but is rejected by the image. When the plate is inked, the ink adheres to the image but is repelled by the damp surface of the remainder of the plate, so that only the image prints.

lower case: small letters as opposed to capitals.

magnetic media: means of storing and transporting encoded information which use a magnetized surface. See *floppy disk*, *hard disk*, and *magnetic tape*.

magnetic tape: tape, either on a reel or in a cassette, used in computers, word processors, and photosetting systems to store and transport encoded programs and text.

make-up: the arrangement of typesetting and illustrations into page form.

mark-up: the process of adding written typographical instructions to a typescript to enable a typesetter to photoset it correctly.

masking: removing or covering portions of an illustration so that they do not appear as part of the printed image.

measure: the width (usually expressed in 12-point ems) to which lines of type are set.

modem: a device which enables text or other computer-generated data to be transmitted by ordinary telephone line to another computer.

offprint: an article or other excerpt from a book or journal run on from the main printing run and often bound separately. See also *reprint*.

offset-lithography: common method of printing by lithography in which the image is first transferred from the plate on to a rubber-covered cylinder whence it is printed on to the paper.

over-running: the transferring of words from one line of type to the next or to the preceding line to accommodate a correction. Such a correction may mean over-running as far as the end of a paragraph. In an extreme case this could affect many subsequent pages.

page proof: a proof made from typesetting which has been divided into pages, with running heads and footnotes in position. This is usually the final proof, on which corrections made to the galley proof can be checked but to which no further alteration should be made.

page-description language: a set of codes of the sort used by desk-top publishing systems and some photosetting systems to store and transmit information.

pagination: the division of text (and illustrations where appropriate) into page lengths. Some photosetting systems can paginate automatically in accordance with rules set by their operators.

parentheses: round brackets ( ).

perfect binding: a method of binding a book or journal without stitching or sewing. The signatures are assembled and their backs cut off. The resulting edge is then covered with an adhesive. Usually a paper cover is attached and the remaining three edges are trimmed. Frequent use of a book bound by this method will normally cause its disintegration.

photolithography: the process of printing by lithography when the plate is prepared photographically from positive or negative film.

photo-offset: offset-lithography where the printing plate has been prepared by a photographic process.

photosetter: a machine which exposes letters on to photographic paper or film, usually by means of a laser beam or a cathode ray tube.

pi character: any character or symbol which is available on a photosetter but is not part of a standard fount.

pica: (1) twelve points. A unit of typographic measurement used in the English-speaking countries. A pica (or 12-point em) is approximately one-sixth of an inch and 'measure' is normally expressed in picas; (2) used in connection with typewriters and word processors, pica is a pitch of 10 characters to the inch.

pitch: when referring to typewriters, or daisy-wheel and dot-matrix printers, the number of characters per inch. The three standard pitches are pica (10 per inch), elite (12 per inch), and micron (15 per inch).

plate: (1) one or more illustrations occupying a page which does not contain part of the continuous text; usually halftone and sometimes printed on different paper from the text; (2) any solid surface which bears an image for printing, commonly by lithography.

point: the basic unit of type measurement in the English-speaking countries, approximately 1/72 inch.

portrait: a book or part of a book (e.g. an illustration or table) which has a height greater than its width. See also *landscape.*

proof: a preliminary copy of text and/or illustrative matter for checking and correction. Not usually an indication of final printed quality. See *galley proof* and *page proof.*

quotes: inverted commas; quotation marks.

range left: set type with beginnings of lines aligned with left-hand margin.

range right: set type with ends of lines aligned with right-hand margin.

raster image processor: rip: a device which converts language designed to describe characters and graphics on a computer screen into instructions suitable for a photosetter or laser printer.

recto: right-hand page: 'start recto' means start on right-hand page.

register: the accurate printing of an impression on a sheet in relation to other impressions already on the sheet; most frequently used with reference to the superimposition of one colour on another. 'Out of register' means that two or more impressions are not correctly aligned.

reprint: a repeat printing without significant alteration. A book reprinted with alterations is called a new edition. 'Reprint' is also sometimes used to mean 'offprint'.

retouching: physically or electronically altering images on photographs, transparencies, or artwork before reproduction.

revise: a revised proof. A second stage of proofing after some corrections have been made.

river: an undesirable space running down several lines of type, caused by wide word-spacing and common in narrow, justified setting.

roman: ordinary upright type, as opposed to *italic* which slants.

rule: a printed straight line.

run on: (1) continue on the same line without paragraph or other break; (2) print a further quantity of sheets, additional to the original order, without stopping the printing machine.

running head: a headline placed at the top of every ordinary text page, stating the title and/or the author of the work or the title of the chapter or section to which that page belongs.

sans serif: typeface without serifs. This is sans serif.

screen: dot pattern in halftone image.

section: (1) signature; (2) part of chapter or article.

serif: a small stroke at the top or bottom of a main stroke of a letter. See also *sans serif.*

set: produce on paper or film characters intended for printing, usually by means of a photosetter; but setting can be done on any equipment the output of which resembles printer's type.

set full out: set to the full type measure; do not indent.

set-off: accidental transfer of ink from one printed sheet to another.

signature: a folded sheet, or part of a sheet, ready for sewing or perfect binding. A signature usually comprises 16 or 32 pages but may be any multiple of 4 up to 64 pages. Also referred to as a section or gathering.

small caps: capital letters of the height and apparent weight of lower-case letters, used in subheadings and running heads, and in traditional book design for the first few words of a chapter or article. THESE ARE SMALL CAPS.

solid: without added space between lines of type. Five lines of 10-point type set solid occupy a depth of 50 points.

solidus: oblique stroke / .

style: rules of an editorial or typographical nature adopted by a printer or publisher to ensure uniformity.

subscript: a small character or symbol which is printed below the base-line of a full-size character. Preferably used to describe diacritical marks centred below the character. See *inferior*.

superior: a small numeral or other character which is printed above the x-height of the normal characters in the text (e.g. a footnote reference number).

superscript: a small character or symbol which is printed above a full-size character (e.g. an accent or diacritical mark).

tip-in: a separately printed leaf pasted (tipped) into a book. Plates, foldouts, and errata slips are often tipped in.

type sizes: measured and denoted by the point system. Common sizes for text use are 8-point, 10-point, 11-point, and 12-point. The point measurement used in the English-speaking countries differs from that used in many other countries. Before about 1880 type sizes were arbitrary and were distinguished by names such as 'nonpareil' and 'bourgeois'.

typeface: a particular type design.

typesetter: one who sets type or the owner of a business which offers a typesetting service.

unjustified: unjustified type has even word spacing, and if, as is usual, it is ranged left, it has a ragged right-hand margin.

vdu: visual display unit: the screen connected to a computer or similar device.

verso: left-hand page: the opposite side of a leaf from the recto.

widow: the short last line of a paragraph when it appears at the top of a page. This is considered undesirable and may be avoided by altering the word spacing to shorten or lengthen the paragraph by one line.

word processor: a device, or computer running a program, designed to facilitate the input and manipulation of text.

wrong fount: the accidental appearance in a piece of typesetting of a character which is of the wrong size or typeface.

x-height: a vertical dimension equal to the height of the lower-case letter *x*, which is the standard height of the lower-case alphabet not including the ascenders and descenders.

15 USEFUL WORKS OF REFERENCE

BS 3700: The Preparation of Indexes for Books, Periodicals, and Other Publications (London: British Standards Institution, 1964)

BS 5261: Guide to Copy Preparation and Proof Correction. Part 1: Recommendations for Preparation of Typescript Copy for Printing (London: British Standards Institution, 1975)

Butcher, Judith, *Copy-Editing: The Cambridge Handbook*, 2nd edn (Cambridge: Cambridge University Press, 1981) [3rd edition to be published 1991]

Hart's Rules for Compositors and Readers at the University Press, Oxford, 39th edn (Oxford: Oxford University Press, 1983)

The Chicago Manual of Style, 13th edn (Chicago: University of Chicago Press, 1982)

The Oxford Writers' Dictionary (Oxford: Oxford University Press, 1990)

16 PROOF CORRECTION

All corrections should be made distinctly in ink in the margins; marks made in the text should be those indicating the place to which the correction refers. An alteration is made by striking through, or marking as indicated in the table below, the character, word, or words to be altered, and writing the new material in the margin, followed by a concluding stroke (/). If several corrections occur in one line they should be divided between the left and right margins, the order being from left to right in each margin; individual marks should be separated by a concluding stroke. When words are changed, deleted, or added it is desirable on a galley proof and essential on a page proof to make changes on adjacent lines to compensate for the space occupied by the characters deleted or added. Otherwise a whole paragraph may have to be reset or pages of type altered as far as the end of the article or chapter.

When checking page proofs it is necessary to ensure not only that each correction marked on the galley proofs has been made, but also that no further errors have been introduced during the process of correction. Running heads and page numbers should be carefully checked on page proofs. It is possible for errors to occur near the head or foot of a page during page make-up; therefore page proofs also should be carefully checked for this. It is often safer to check these points as a separate operation after reading through the page proofs in the normal way.

Normally only matter to be substituted for, or added to, the existing text should be written on the proof. If, however, there are any problems or comments to be brought to the attention of the printer, they should be written on the proof, encircled, and preceded by the word 'PRINTER' (in capitals).

The following table of proof correction marks is based on Part 2 of *Guide to Copy Preparation and Proof Correction* (*BS 5261*, Part 2, 1976) and material from this publication is reproduced by permission of the British Standards Institution, 2 Park Street, London W1A 2BS, from whom complete copies may be obtained.

Group A General

Number	Instruction	Textual mark	Marginal mark	Notes
A1	Correction is concluded	None	/	Make after each correction
A2	Leave unchanged	— — — — — — under characters to remain	√ (circled)	
A3	Remove extraneous marks	Encircle marks to be removed	✕	e.g. film or paper edges visible between lines on bromide or diazo proofs
A3.1	Push down spacing material which has risen and printed between words or lines	Encircle blemish	⊥	
A4	Refer to appropriate authority anything of doubtful accuracy	Encircle word(s) affected	(?)	

Group B Deletion, insertion and substitution

B1	Insert in text the matter indicated in the margin	ʎ	New matter followed by ʎ	Indentical to B2
B2	Insert additional matter identified by a letter in a diamond	ʎ	ʎ Followed by for example ◇A	The additional copy should be supplied with the corresponding letter marked on it in a diamond e.g. ◇A
B3	Delete	/ through character(s) or ├———┤ through words to be deleted	∂	
B4	Delete and close up	/ through character or ├———┤ through characters e.g. chara͡cter chara͜ecter	∂ (with close-up marks)	

Number	Instruction	Textual mark	Marginal mark	Notes
B5	Substitute character or substitute part of one or more word(s)	/ through character or ⊢————⊣ through word(s)	New character or new word(s)	
B6	Wrong fount. Replace by character(s) of correct fount	Encircle character(s) to be changed	⊗	
B6.1	Change damaged character(s)	Encircle character(s) to be changed	✕	This mark is identical to A3
B7	Set in or change to italic	———— under character(s) to be set or changed	⊔⊔	Where space does not permit textual marks encircle the affected area instead
B8	Set in or change to capital letters	≡≡≡ under character(s) to be set or changed	≡	
B9	Set in or change to small capital letters	══ under character(s) to be set or changed	══	
B9.1	Set in or change to capital letters for initial letters and small capital letters for the rest of the words	≡ under initial letters and ══ under rest of the word(s)	══	
B10	Set in or change to bold type	∿∿∿∿ under character(s) to be set or changed	∿	
B11	Set in or change to bold italic type	∿∿∿∿ under character(s) to be set or changed	⊔⊔∿	
B12	Change capital letters to lower case letters	Encircle character(s) to be changed	≢	For use when B5 is inappropriate

Number	Instruction	Textual mark	Marginal mark	Notes
B12.1	Change small capital letters to lower case letters	Encircle character(s) to be changed	≠	For use when B5 is inappropriate
B13	Change italic to upright type	Encircle character(s) to be changed	�	
B14	Invert type	Encircle character to be inverted	◠	
B15	Substitute or insert character in 'superior' position	/ through character or ʎ where required	⌐ under character e.g. 2	
B16	Substitute or insert character in 'inferior' position	/ through character or ʎ where required	L over character e.g. 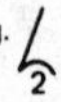 /₂	
B17	Substitute ligature e.g. fh for separate letters	⊢———⊣ through characters affected	‿ e.g. 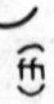 fh	
B17.1	Substitute separate letters for ligature	⊢———⊣	Write out separate letters	
B18	Substitute or insert full stop or decimal point	/ through character or ʎ where required	⊙	
B18.1	Substitute or insert colon	/ through character or ʎ where required	 ⊙	
B18.2	Substitute or insert semi-colon	/ through character or ʎ where required	;	

Number	Instruction	Textual mark	Marginal mark	Notes
B18.3	Substitute or insert comma	/ through character or ʌ where required	ʔ	
B18.4	Substitute or insert apostrophe	/ through character or ʌ where required	ʼ⁷	
B18.5	Substitute or insert single quotation marks	/ through character or ʌ where required	ʻ⁷ and/or ʼ⁷	
B18.6	Substitute or insert double quotation marks	/ through character or ʌ where required	ʻʻ⁷ and/or ʼʼ⁷	
B19	Substitute or insert ellipsis	/ through character or ʌ where required	• • •	
B20	Substitute or insert leader dots	/ through character or ʌ where required	(• • •)	Give the measure of the leader when necessary
B21	Substitute or insert hyphen	/ through character or ʌ where required	⊢⊣	
B22	Substitute or insert rule	/ through character ʌ where required	⊢⊣	Give the size of the rule in the marginal mark e.g. ⊢ 1 em ⊣ ⊢ 4 mm ⊣

Number	Instruction	Textual mark	Marginal mark	Notes
B23	Substitute or insert oblique	/ through character or ⋀ where required		

Group C Positioning and spacing

Number	Instruction	Textual mark	Marginal mark	Notes
C1	Start new paragraph			
C2	Run on (no new paragraph)			
C3	Transpose characters or words	between characters or words, numbered when necessary		
C4	Transpose a number of characters or words	3 2 1	1 2 3	To be used when the sequence cannot be clearly indicated by the use of C3. The vertical strokes are made through the characters or words to be transposed and numbered in the correct sequence
C5	Transpose lines			
C6	Transpose a number of lines		—— 3 —— 2 —— 1	To be used when the sequence cannot be clearly indicated by C5. Rules extend from the margin into the text with each line to be transplanted numbered in the correct sequence
C7.	Centre	enclosing matter to be centred	[ ]	
C8	Indent			Give the amount of the indent in the marginal mark

Number	Instruction	Textual mark	Marginal mark	Notes
C9	Cancel indent			
C10	Set line justified to specified measure	and/or		Give the exact dimensions when necessary
C11	Set column justified to specified measure			Give the exact dimensions when necessary
C12	Move matter specified distance to the right	enclosing matter to be moved to the right		Give the exact dimensions when necessary
C13	Move matter specified distance to the left	enclosing matter to be moved to the left		Give the exact dimensions when necessary
C14	Take over character(s), word(s) or line to next line, column or page			The textual mark surrounds the matter to be taken over and extends into the margin
C15	Take back character(s), word(s), or line to previous line, column or page			The textual mark surrounds the matter to be taken back and extends into the margin
C16	Raise matter	over matter to be raised / under matter to be raised		Give the exact dimensions when necessary. (Use C28 for insertion of space between lines or paragraphs in text)
C17	Lower matter	over matter to be lowered / under matter to be lowered		Give the exact dimensions when necessary. (Use C29 for reduction of space between lines or paragraphs in text)
C18	Move matter to position indicated	Enclose matter to be moved and indicate new position		Give the exact dimensions when necessary

Number	Instruction	Textual mark	Marginal mark	Notes
C19	Correct vertical alignment	‖	‖	
C20	Correct horizontal alignment	Single line above and below misaligned matter e.g. mi_saligned	—	The marginal mark is placed level with the head and foot of the relevant line
C21	Close up. Delete space between characters or words	linking ⌣ characters	⌣	
C22	Insert space between characters	| between characters affected	Y	Give the size of the space to be inserted when necessary
C23	Insert space between words	Y between words affected	Y	Give the size of the space to be inserted when necessary
C24	Reduce space between characters	| between characters affected	⋂	Give the amount by which the space is to be reduced when necessary
C25	Reduce space between words	⋂ between words affected	⋂	Give amount by which the space is to be reduced when necessary
C26	Make space appear equal between characters or words	| between characters or words affected	Ⴤ	
C27	Close up to normal interline spacing	(each side of column linking lines)		The textual marks extend into the margin

Number	Instruction	Textual mark	Marginal mark	Notes
C28	Insert space between lines or paragraphs			The marginal mark extends between the lines of text. Give the size of the space to be inserted when necessary
C29	Reduce space between lines or paragraphs			The marginal mark extends between the lines of text. Give the amount by which the space is to be reduced when necessary

MARKS TO BE MADE ON PROOF, OR PROOFS, AFTER READING

MARK	MEANING
'Revise' (and signature)	Correct and submit another proof.
'Revise and make-up' (and signature)	Correct and submit another proof in page form.
'Revise and press' (and signature)	Make final corrections and print off without submitting another proof.
'Press' (and signature)	No correction necessary. The work may be printed.

Marked galley proof of text

(B9.1)   =/   At the sign of the red pale   Y/

(B13)   山/   *The Life and Work of William Caxton, by H W Larken*

(C7)   [ ]/   [An Extract]   ∿/

(C9)   ⌐/   Few people, even in the field of printing, have any clear   =/
conception of what William Caxton did or, indeed, of
what he was. Much of this lack of knowledge is due to the
absence of information that can be counted as factual
and the consequent tendency to vague generalisation.

(B12)   ≠/   Though it is well known that Caxton was born in the
county of Kent, there is no information as to the precise

(B18.5)   ✓/   place. In his prologue to the *History of Troy*, William Caxton   ✓/
wrote 'for in France I was never and was born and   .../
learned my English in Kent in the Weald where I doubt

(B18.5)   ✓/   not is spoken as broad and rude English as in any place   Y/
of England.' During the fifteenth century there were a

(B6)   Ⓚ/   great number of Flemish cloth weavers in Kent; most
of them had come to England at the instigation of
Edward III with the object of teaching their craft to the

(B17)   f̂l/   English. So successful was this venture that the English   t/
cloth trade flourished and the agents who sold the cloth   ∂/

(C8)   ⌐/   (the mercers) became very wealthy people. There have be
There have been many speculations concerning the origin
of the Caxton family and much research has been carried
out. It is assumed often that Caxton's family must have   ⌐/

(B14)   ∩/   been connected with the wool trade in order to have
secured his apprenticeship to an influential merchant.

(A4)   ⑦/   W. Blyth Crotch (*Prologues and Epilogues of William*   Ш/
(B7)   Ш/   *Caxton*) suggests that the origin of the name Caxton (of
which there are several variations in spelling) may be
traced to Cambridgeshire but notes that many writers
have suggested that Caxton was connected with a family

(A3.1)   ⊥/   at Hadlow or alternatively a family in Canterbury. =/
(B18.1)   ⊙/   Of the Canterbury connection a William Caxton
became freeman of the City in 1431 and William Pratt,
a mercer who was the printer's friend, was born there.

(B15)   ✓/   H. R. Plomer suggests that Pratt and Caxton might possibly
have been schoolboys together, perhaps at the school St.
Alphege. In this parish there lived a John Caxton who

(C26)   Ⴤ/   used as his mark three cakes over a barrell (or tun) and   ⋀Ⓐ/
who is mentioned in an inscription on a monument in
the church of St. Alphege.

In 1941, Alan Keen (an authority on manuscripts) XI (A3)
secured some documents concerning Caxton; these are
now in the BRITISH MUSEUM. Discovered in the library of ≠I (B12.1)
Earl Winterton at Shillinglee Park by Richard Holworthy,
the documents cover the period 1420 to 1467. One of
Winterton's ancestors purchased the manor of West
Wratting from a family named Caxton, the property
being situated in the Weald of Kent.

There is also record of a property mentioning Philip I (C2)
Caxton and his wife Dennis who had two sons, Philip I (B4)
(born in 1413) and William

Particularly interesting in these documents is one
recording that Philip Caxton junior sold the manor of
Little Wratting to John Christemasse of London in 1436, 1e HI (B22)
the deed having been witnessed by two aldermen, one of I (C14)
whom was Robert Large, the printer's employer.
Further, in 1439, the other son, William Caxton, con HI (B21)
Wratting to John Christemasse, and an indenture of 1457 —2
concerning this property mentions one William Caxton —3 I (C6)
veyed his rights in the manor Bluntes Hall at Little —1
alias Causton. It is an interesting coincidence to note that
the lord of the manor of Little Wratting was the father of
Margaret, Duchess of Burgundy. TI (C25)
In 1420, a Thomas Caxton of Tenterden witnessed the (+1pt (C28)
will of a fellow townsman; he owned property in Kent and
appears to have been a person of some importance.
)−1pt (C29)

[1] See 'William Caxton'.

Ⓐ attached to Christchurch Monastery in the parish of

17 INDEX